5/16/2022

Dear

Congratulations on your graduation and your achievements.

May Our Lord bless you as you continue to acquire and develop the wisdom and perseverance to accomplish your life's dreams.

Love,
Uncle Thy

Finding My Purpose, Finding My Way in Life

DISCOVERING THE PATH TO ACHIEVE MY DREAMS

J. O. GONZALEZ

WESTBOW
PRESS®
A DIVISION OF THOMAS NELSON
& ZONDERVAN

Copyright © 2022 J. O. Gonzalez.

All rights reserved. No part of this book may be used or reproduced by any means, graphic, electronic, or mechanical, including photocopying, recording, taping or by any information storage retrieval system without the written permission of the author except in the case of brief quotations embodied in critical articles and reviews.

WestBow Press books may be ordered through booksellers or by contacting:

WestBow Press
A Division of Thomas Nelson & Zondervan
1663 Liberty Drive
Bloomington, IN 47403
www.westbowpress.com
844-714-3454

Because of the dynamic nature of the Internet, any web addresses or links contained in this book may have changed since publication and may no longer be valid. The views expressed in this work are solely those of the author and do not necessarily reflect the views of the publisher, and the publisher hereby disclaims any responsibility for them.

Any people depicted in stock imagery provided by Getty Images are models, and such images are being used for illustrative purposes only. Certain stock imagery © Getty Images.

Interior Image Credit: J O Gonzalez

Scripture taken from the King James Version of the Bible.

ISBN: 978-1-6642-5131-1 (sc)
ISBN: 978-1-6642-5132-8 (hc)
ISBN: 978-1-6642-5130-4 (e)

Library of Congress Control Number: 2021924088

Print information available on the last page.

WestBow Press rev. date: 12/29/2021

CONTENTS

Introduction ix

Chapter 1	My Journey as a Student Begins	1
Chapter 2	Finding and Defining Our Purpose	15
Chapter 3	Imagination, Dreams, and Aspirations	29
Chapter 4	Organized Planning	39
Chapter 5	Execution of the Plan	50
Chapter 6	Staying Focused	63
Chapter 7	The Stages of Life	72
Chapter 8	Remain Teachable	82
Chapter 9	Giving Back	91
Chapter 10	Living Your Life Full of Joy	102
Chapter 11	Believe	115

References 121

To my mother, Julia Maria Zayas Gonzalez; my daughters, Guimazoa and Rosemarie; my grandchildren, Xaris, Abimael, and Winter, and to my wife, Wanda.

God's love is forever. He is the most powerful force in the universe. Because of God's love, He made all things in the universe. Because He loved us so much, He gave His only Son, Jesus Christ, so that you and I—and all of us who believe in Him—shall not perish but have everlasting life (John 3:16 KJV). Amen. The Word has become real in my life.

Grandfather and grandson

Train up a child in the way he should go: and when he is old, he will not depart from it.
—Proverbs 22:6

INTRODUCTION

Purpose is defined in different ways. The *Oxford Languages Dictionary* says it is "the reason for which something is done or created or for which something exists." *Merriam Webster* defines purpose as "something set up as an object or end to be attained."

What does "defining my purpose" mean? It means discovering who I am and what things I can be and do in my life.

Defining something implies a process of discovery. It requires that I invest time and effort to research the possibilities. It means seeking to be the best I can be by discovering what I am here to do. What is my contribution to the universe?

It means doing the best I can with what I've got every day. It means competing with myself to be better every day, one day at a time. It means performing at the best level I can to deliver the results I seek. In order to perform to the best of my abilities, I must know what those skills and abilities are.

I must know why I want to make an effort to realize my potential and maximize these abilities. Does it mean I have to deliver all A's all the time in all subjects, as a student, in all classes? It does not necessarily mean all A's. Does it mean that I am constantly comparing to the results that others produced? Not necessarily. What matters is that I can learn about what I can do well and with joy. The most important outcomes in my life are what I learn, how I improve, how I become the best version of me, and how I serve others as who I am and with what I have.

Does it mean I have to go to college to be successful? Not necessarily. I have many choices.

My goal with this book is to help you identify your choices and help you make decisions about what you want to become in the future. It should be a combination of God's will, your God-given will, your talents, and the desires, dreams, and aspirations of your heart.

As the cover image communicates—with an image that can be compared to life itself—life has many alternatives, roads, and directions to follow. The right path could be to follow a straight course or go to the right or the left. How do we know for sure? The sunlight and the blue sky mean hope and goodness that we can find when we seek to reach our objectives and enjoy the trip during the process.

My objective with this book is to share ideas with you and stimulate your minds and your heart. Perhaps you have read or experienced some of these ideas. The subjects addressed here are not new or groundbreaking. During the following chapters, I will share some of my personal experiences about learning and growing. I will also bring to the discussion the experiences of many other individuals—all experts on their fields—to reach out to the innermost places of your minds and heart. During this process of sharing ideas and experiences, I aim to help you discover and develop your potential, define your purpose, and determine how to make it become your reality.

How important is to find a purpose for my life? I hope that I am able to answer this and other important questions. Most importantly, I hope you are able to answer this question for yourself. If you decide to be a student of whatever subject you choose, remember that you have choices, you are capable, and you already have what it takes. All you have to do is believe it, imagine it, decide to do it, plan it, and take action.

If you work hard, you will overcome any obstacles you find. We are all students in life; even before we were born, we were learning.

The learning process ends when our lives on this planet come to an end.

Finding your purpose is a very personal endeavor. It is not something that anyone can do for you. It is a personal quest. It requires seeking to communicate with the Lord via a life of prayer, fasting, and studying the Word. The ideas will come, and the Lord will provide everything you need to realize your purpose. He is the Creator of all things. In the beginning, He created all the resources required for humans to fulfill our purpose.

May the Lord use this humble servant and this writing to help you walk through life and serve Him by serving others and being a great steward of all the things the Lord will place on your hands.

A path through green vegetation

Trust in the Lord with all your heart and lean not on your own understanding. In all ways, acknowledge Him, and He shall direct your paths.
—Proverbs 3:5–6

CHAPTER 1

My Journey as a Student Begins

Learning is a lifelong journey, and it starts early in life. From birth, we really are students of our environment, our circumstances, and the universe around us. In fact, in a recent TED presentation, Annie Murphy Paul,[10] discusses how even before we are born, we are learning. By the time we are on the third trimester in our mothers' wombs, our auditory systems are functional, and we are able to hear and learn our mothers' speaking sounds. We are then able to recognize these sounds, which then become familiar. Even the emotional state of the mother influences the learning of the fetus and may have long-term effects on the child.

Every moment, all our senses are absorbing and collecting information about what is going on around us, and this is how we begin to form an image in our minds of how things are or should be. Many times, we collect information from negative sources that feed us incorrect information; however, when we believe the source of the information, we accept the information as fact, and it becomes true in our minds. This is happening throughout our lives and occurs until the end of our journeys on this planet. It may slow down during our later years, but the process is at work every day, in every moment, and in each experience.

As we grow and achieve a certain level of consciousness and

understanding, we are then able to make choices that lead toward paths in life. Some of us start early in assuming responsibility for the choices that take us to the paths we choose. Some individuals never take responsibility for the choices they make.

I did not know this at the time, but when I was a child, I took destructive paths in life. It actually took me years to understand the fact that I needed to learn to develop confidence in my ability to learn in order to grow as an individual and fulfill my purpose in life. Terri Apter,[2] author of *The Confident Child*, writes that the best way to help our children develop confidence and achieve their full potential in life is to help them develop self-esteem. She writes that self-esteem has a far greater impact than intelligence or innate ability. Children who believe that they are valuable and effective—and who have the skills to behave in accord with these beliefs—have higher expectations of future success, persist longer in tasks, and show higher levels of overall performance than other children who are equally able but less confident. Emotional intelligence, which is a crucial part of self-esteem, gives children resilience and enables them to tolerate frustration and engage in sustained effort. This special form of intelligence also involves awareness of how their behavior affects other people, thereby inspiring concern for others and responsibility for their actions (17–18).

Kevin Cashman, author of *Leadership from the Inside Out*, writes about emotional intelligence as "two interactive qualities of emotional intelligence: awareness of self and awareness of others" (25). Awareness is to achieve understanding. It is realization. It is to have a clear picture or image in our minds of who we are and what and who is surrounding us. It is having knowledge and consciousness of our roles and the roles of others. It is gaining knowledge through our own perceptions of ourselves, our surroundings, and others around us. Through the development of emotional intelligence, we are able to sense situations and be considerate with ourselves and others.

Self-esteem is our sense of our own value and our own worth.

- Finding My Purpose, Finding My Way in Life -

It is a set of skills that helps us develop the strengths and necessary resolve to continue to move forward toward the attainment of our goals, dreams, and aspirations in the face of obstacles and difficulties. Positive self-esteem allows us to continue to move forward learning and improving day in and day out for all our lives (Apter 1997).

Therefore, self-esteem and emotional intelligence are intimately related, and both start developing early in our lives. However, we can always go back and reinvent ourselves and take actions to improve—no matter what stage of life we are in. We must continue to look for answers and find our way into an improved self and toward the realization of our purpose in life.

In 1952, I was born in the newly built hospital of the city of Villalba. This municipality had two coffee plantations. One of them, La Hacienda El Limon, owned by Mr. and Mrs. Walter McJones, was where my mother was born.

After World War II, the Philippines obtained its independence. In the 1950s, Hawaii and Alaska became states. However, Puerto Rico officially became the commonwealth of Puerto Rico via US Congress Law 600 of 1952. It was also during the Korean War. Soon thereafter, transformation on the island of Puerto Rico got underway. Operation Bootstrap (*Manos a la Obra*) started, and the commonwealth moved toward an improved quality of life, including a better health system, better education, and a revolution in light industrial development, tourism, and retailing. I was part of that transformation.

My mother was a tremendous influence in my life. She was the best Sunday school teacher in the universe. Through her Sunday school classes in the early seventies, she educated a group of about thirty kids, and through these efforts, she helped most of them find purpose in their lives. From this humble Sunday school class in the house, she was rebuilding after her retirement from more than thirty years of public service work. A Christian congregation was reborn, and the United Church of Christ of the Romero Ward in the small mountain town of Villalba, Puerto Rico, was reestablished. My mother learned the art of teaching from her father. I graduated from Francisco Zayas Santana High School, which was named after my grandfather. My mother's father was the first teacher from Villalba. I am very proud of my family. What a great heritage of teaching and serving!

The process of rebuilding this congregation—buildings and all—was a tough uphill battle. However, my mother's dream was realized through determination, hard work, faith, and the help of many godsent angels. Her faith in herself and in Jesus Christ our Lord made it possible to build a new church building to worship. Later on, we built classrooms to teach practical Christianity. More importantly, from this effort, the rebuilding of a congregation of families took place. They were uplifted, and many generations continue to serve the Lord.

Many pastors, professionals, and other leaders were developed because of this effort. This project was made real—born out of my mother's dream, hope, and vision. With no resources to speak of, the resources came and became physical because she believed and placed her faith into action. Others believed because she believed.

She taught me to read and encouraged me to read at an early age. She also dragged me to church when I was a little kid and helped me understand God's gift of love and life everlasting.

Later on, my father and mother went to live in the great city of Ponce, and I followed. I spent time with them and learned to love this beautiful, historic city on the south of the island of Puerto Rico by the Caribbean Sea.

I was a student at *Segunda Unidad*—Jose Gonzalez Ginorio School, Romero Ward, Villalba, from first grade to ninth grade. This rural school had an elementary school program and a junior high school program. I have some great memories from those years. I also experienced challenging moments and growing pains during those years. Nevertheless, that school was full of magic and wonders. I was learning languages, history, science, mathematics, social studies, and economics through the windows that were the books we used and through the eyes and minds of my teachers.

The school was across the street from *El Lago Guayabal*. Lake Guayabal was formed by the construction of a dam at the intersection of the Jacaguas and Toa Vaca Rivers in 1913 by the Puerto Rico Power Authority with the assistance of the US Geological Service and the US Department of Interior, among other institutions. The intersection of these two rivers, at that point, also marked the border dividing the municipalities of Juana Diaz and Villalba. The rivers came down from the Central Mountain Range, running north to south. The lake's purpose was to irrigate the croplands in the southern coastal plains of the island. The lake supported a major irrigation infrastructure to help improve the island's main industry at the time (1958): agriculture (PUBS.USGS.GOV 2013). For all of us as small children, *el lago* (the lake) was an incredible spectacle of water, life, beauty, danger, and mystery. On one occasion, we were confronted with death when two soldiers stationed at nearby Fort Allen drowned. We witnessed the authorities conducting the search on the lake. We were told the soldiers' boat accidentally capsized during a fishing trip. It affected my schoolmates and me very much. I could not comprehend why people died.

As first and second graders, we were very impressionable. Many, many times, we watched a small yellow biplane fly really low over the lake. It would come during the planting of the sugarcane fields across the lake. It would spray herbicides and other chemicals on the sugarcane fields just north of the lake. We would watch with amazement as this beautiful aircraft twisted and turned while spraying the fields. On occasion, the pilot would come low over the lake after he was finished, and it would seem the plane was going to hit the dam structure until the plane gained altitude at the last minute and went over the dam. We could see the pilot and wave, and he would wave back at us. What a sight! It was very impressive to me. Who would have thought that the memory of those moments would stay so clear and crisp in the mind of this small boy all his life? Some impressions and images—in incredible detail—stay with us forever. My senses were recording every experience mixed with emotions, and I was learning.

During the late 1950s, sugarcane, coffee, and tobacco made up about 90 percent of our economy on this beautiful Caribbean island paradise. The sugarcane industry produced refined sugar and fueled the production of famous rum brands, such as Don Q, Barrilito, Ron Llave, and Bacardi. The southern city of Yauco became the center of coffee production, and the famous Yaucono premium coffee became well-known all over Europe. Cigar production was big in the mountain town of Cayey with the huge Consolidated Cigar Company. My father's father and mother owned and operated a small cigar factory, which produced cigars that were sold to Consolidated Cigar.

In the north, the Caribe Hilton Hotel was being built in San Juan, and the Rockefellers owned Cerromar Beach Hotel and Golf Resort facing the majestic Atlantic Ocean, which were powerful evidence of a growing tourism industry. I learned these facts in school. During social studies, we discussed the economy, government, and other related topics. I was at school when we received word that President Kennedy had been shot and killed. We were all devastated by this sad news. *How can this happen? Who killed him?*

At the lake, my cousins, and I went fishing many times, mostly on very quiet afternoons. At this time, the sun was setting, the heat of the day was slowly fading, and the fish would come closer to the surface and bite more than at any other time of the day. At this time, the silence and beauty stimulated our senses. We could sometimes hear music playing from across the lake. It was the early sixties, and I was introduced to beautiful songs through this music far in the distance. My interest in music was born, and I was learning.

My first grade teacher was a beautiful young lady. She was amazing. I was amazed by her looks and her sweet way of relating to me. We did not have kindergarten in those days. Education started in first grade. She patiently worked with me to teach me to write

- Finding My Purpose, Finding My Way in Life -

my complete name: first name, middle name, and then my two last names. I looked around and realized that each child in my class had their own story. We had very smart kids and others who were slow. Some came to school wearing dirty clothes or broken shoes. I slowly learned I was blessed with neat and clean uniforms and good shoes.

I participated in plays and dance presentations at various moments in first, second, and third grades and continued until higher grades. I had fun with those experiences. We had a first grade graduation ceremony, and I received good grades. I was an honors student. My life as a student was progressing to another stage. I learned that my mother was an important and respected person in the Education Department at the local level and that my father was a famous automotive specialist and enthusiast. He was a craftsman and loved Ford vehicles. I felt I was living up to the challenge of being the son of such great individuals.

I had many great learning experiences and several great teachers in school. However, my two best teachers during my years at Jose Gonzalez Ginorio School—the ones who impacted me the most—were my English teacher and my science teacher during junior high. They were both really interested and had a genuine interest in my learning outcome with these subjects and our application of their subjects in general. My graduation from junior high was an important event, and I was one of the top students in the class. I was not involved in sports, except baseball, and I learned to love this sport.

I was a very good student, and I was learning.

During high, I read the only historical novel of Puerto Rico, *Isla Cerrera* (Wild (Uncivilized) Island), by Manuel Mendez Ballester, a famous Puerto Rican author. This story has many similarities to the story of Pocahontas in North America. Many stories like this probably took place in North, South, and Central America since idealistic Europeans were captivated and fell in love with beautiful and smart native women.

The story starts on or about 1509 when Juan Ponce de Leon

went to Puerto Rico to start the development of the island, under directions from the king and queen of Spain. I read it many more times after that, and I felt in *love* with the characters, particularly Guimazoa, its female leading character, and Ricardo de Boadilla, a young Spanish conqueror who was the main character.

Ricardo de Boadilla had dreams of accomplishing extraordinary things in life. He struggled with his Christian upbringing and the cruel realities of civilizing the indigenous Taino population. Like Ricardo de Boadilla, I too had dreams of conquests in life and doing extraordinary things. I did not know exactly what conquests I was going to face or attempt, but I was convinced that I was a conqueror.

Isla Cerrera came alive for me in my mind. The images described by the author became real for me, and I named one of my daughters after a female character. What an influence a good book can have on a child's mind! A good book can give us a lasting impression of what others have seen and experienced. All my senses were capturing information from my experiences and from the experiences of others through their writings. I was learning a great many things.

At Francisco Zayas Santana High School, I had great teachers—and others who were not so great. I clearly remember my first test at Villalba High. It was a biology test, and I got 100 percent. Some of my classmates were impressed, including a beautiful girl named Suzy. I fell in wildly love with her right away. I lived for many years with terrible emotions because I realized I did not treat her the right way. These emotions are very powerful.

I moved around quite a bit and spent my growing years in the city of Ponce. Life in Ponce was great: Union Street, Buenos Aires Street with my beautiful cousins, Clausell's neighborhood, La Ceiba residential project, Barrio Cotto Laurel, Valle Alto Development. Ponce was always hot with blue skies, beautiful all around, with the cathedral, the historic fire station, the plazas, the shopping centers, movie theaters, and Ponce High School—with my beautiful long-haired neighbor. The great La Sonora Ponceña—with its magic

- Finding My Purpose, Finding My Way in Life -

musical sound and swing and very popular sounds of the era—was a great Latin band.

Turmoil started to rock my life when I started high school, and I was not prepared for what was to come. Soon after I started high school, my life began to go through a series of turbulent periods. By that time, it had been three years since my parents had divorced. My father had started his own business and was doing quite well. My mother, on the other hand, was struggling for survival, day in and day out. They both moved on in life, but I stayed behind with my grandparents in the neighborhood where I grew up. I was moving from one foggy situation to another. There were many things I could not understand. I experienced periods of confusion and anger. I was losing my concept of who I was, and I felt like I was walking on shaky ground.

Even though I was struggling emotionally and had not performed to the best of my abilities, some of my teachers recognized my potential. During my senior year at Villalba High, I was given the opportunity to attend the Center for Educational Opportunities (CROEM) in Las Mesas, Mayaguez, Puerto Rico. It was an effort of the commonwealth's Department of Education, with assistance from the US Department of Education, to promote the studies of languages, English and Spanish, mathematics, and sciences. The center had a special relationship with our neighbor, the University of Puerto Rico, College of Engineering and Mechanical Arts.

The facilities of the center were on an old Air Force communications base sitting at the top of *El Cerro Las Mesas*, a mountain to the east of the city of Mayaguez, at the westernmost part of the island. We had fantastic, beautiful views on a clear day. The air force had given this land back to the state after it no longer had a need for it. As the Cold War slowly moved toward the end, the nearby Ramey Air Force Base, home of a squadron of B-52 long-range bombers was closed, and the communications outpost was no longer needed.

My learning at the educational center was a great experience. I met a lot of great people, fell in love, studied music, and played on a fifteen-piece swinging musical big band. I was the bass player. I was engaged in mastering my reading skills in English and Spanish and getting into reading in a big way. I enjoyed English literature, including Charles Dickens's *A Tale of Two Cities* and Spanish literature. Including Miguel de Cervantes Saavedra's *Don Quix*ote. I enjoyed other literary classics like *The Count of Monte Cristo* by Alexander Dumas and *La Llamarada* of Enrique Laguerre.

I became accomplished in math and science: algebra, trigonometry, geometry, physics, and biology. However, did not do very well in chemistry. I also did well in history: History of the World, History of Civilizations, History of the United States of America, and History of Puerto Rico. Reading about history became a passion. I was somewhat conscious of the fact that I had several paths I could choose to follow in life, but I was insecure and was not confident in following any one path in particular. I wanted to close my eyes and wake up later on to a better life and fulfillment. I did not know how to get from here to there, and I kept searching.

Even though this was a great learning opportunity, I was in a downward spiral of low self-esteem and lack of purpose that would eventually manifest itself in failures and poor performance. We lose battles in life for different reasons, but we often lose because we believe that we cannot win. We can have a distorted image of who we are and believe we do not deserve to win. Losing and poor performance have an impact on self-image. This tends to create an emotional state of little or no hope in our minds. This happened to me by the time I finished high school. This state of confusion did not happen overnight. It was a process, an accumulation of experiences, which led into the wrong paths.

I continued to experience turbulent times because of my personal situation and the struggle my parents were experiencing, each of them in their own way. For some reason, not having a family was my fault; therefore, I was not deserving of anything good in life.

I walked into college without a plan, confused, sad, mad, and looking for something I did not know what it was. I was in denial of who I was and my circumstances. In college, I found sex, alcohol, marijuana, cocaine and other drugs, and the seduction of music in a big way. The first event in college was an orientation program where we were told to look at the person in front of you, beside you, and behind you. Four out of five were going to fail. This is what we were told. I did not know these people were planting thoughts of failure in our minds. What a terrible way to greet young students! This was very negative, and I believed the negative message was for me. I was learning negative and incorrect things.

In *The 7 Habits of Highly Effective Teens*, Sean Covey wrote, "Habit 1 is to be proactive—take responsibility for your life and habit 2 is to begin with the end in mind—define your mission and goals in life."

It took me several significant failures and a long time to comprehend these principles.

I had very little confidence in my abilities to do anything worthwhile in life. I blamed my parents, my friends, and everything else, including the weather, for my circumstances. I had no idea that I could change my circumstances and change my life. I was not able to find a good example, a mentor, to hang on to. I am not sure why. Perhaps I did not make a real effort or look hard enough.

I remember the teachers who were truly dedicated to their profession and helped me alone my learning journey. Unfortunately, I can say that a significant number of my teachers since the beginning of my learning experience—from first grade all the way to my master's degree, while stopping at seven great universities—were not very interested on my learning experience. I never assumed responsibility for my life and my learning experience until later in my life as a young adult. It took me years to learn. At some point along the journey, I learned that it was my responsibility to learn and be a good student—regardless of who was teaching or guiding. The responsibility, I discovered, was mine, and I had to find out what I needed to learn and demonstrate my achievement.

I went on with my life. As I developed, I became a bilingual, educated *jibaro* from Villalba, via the great city of Ponce and the great city of Chicago. I watched as the island in the Caribbean where I was born was transformed into an industrial, educated, confused island paradise of beautiful people.

I went on to the US mainland and became a warrior. I was one of the last of the "draftees" at the end of the Vietnam era. I was a member of the Seventh Special Forces Group, Signal Company, Support Battalion, United States Army, as a communications security specialist. This was a great experience. I was surrounded by extraordinary people. I learned and traveled.

I went on to learn a great deal about computers, business management, and leadership. I continued my learning experience and enjoyed every step of the way.

For many years I wondered why I was not able to find direction in my life and develop a real sense of what was possible. For many years after my late teens, young adult, and early mature years, I was foggy in terms of what I wanted to accomplish or even who I was. I allowed circumstances to derail my pursuit of happiness and higher achievements. Then I realized and asked, *What does it take to be the best I can be? What does it take to develop my full potential?*

As Buck Rogers, former marketing vice president of IBM affirmed and presented, we need to be on good terms with ourselves. We must have peace in our hearts and be able to live this moment today by focusing on the task at hand and giving our best to our efforts. We must know what we want to accomplish. What is our ultimate goal? What do we want to do today, tomorrow, and the next day? We need to know what is required to obtain what we are looking for. We need to know what resources, tools, and individuals or institutions we require to obtain what we seek.

During my early years, I did not know who I was or what I wanted to do. I wanted to be a pilot, an astronaut, an engineer, a musician, a millionaire, a soldier, a banker, an investor, and none of

- Finding My Purpose, Finding My Way in Life -

the above. I did not understand that I had to make a decision and do and be one thing—and do it well.

Therefore, learn this fundamental truth: We must make a decision about what we want to do in life to earn a living. No one can make this decision for us. It is our responsibility. It is perhaps the second most important decision we will ever make. The earlier in life we are able to do it, the better. However, it is never too late.

Get into reading—you will gain knowledge from the experiences of others.

Appreciate your teachers and those around you who are showing you the way; they are passing on a treasure of knowledge to you.

Open your eyes to what is happening around you and absorb and enjoy every moment—even when you face difficulties and challenges.

Make a decision about what you want to do with your life—the earlier, the better.

Then take action; it is your life and your responsibility.

Child warrior preparing for life

Have I not commanded you? Be strong and of good
courage; do not be afraid, nor be dismayed, for the
Lord your God is with you wherever you go.
—Joshua 1:9

CHAPTER 2

Finding and Defining Our Purpose

Merriam Webster defines purpose as "something set up as an objective or an end to be." It is intimately related to intention which is defined as "a determination to act in a certain way." It is why we are who we are and why we act the way we act. It is what moves us to choose a certain path in life and not another. It is an idea, a collection of thoughts in our minds and in our hearts, that propels us to move forward and overcome obstacles and difficulties.

If we have a big purpose, we will achieve extraordinary things in life. If we have a small purpose, our achievements will be small. A big achievement is not better than a small achievement. The important thing is that we achieve the purpose that moves us and what we set out to be and do. Defining purpose is a very personal matter. It is a choice and discovery that we need to make on our own. We need the help of others along the way, but the decisions are ours.

Part of the process of discovering and defining our purpose is to identify and recognize our gifts. Talents and gifts are the skills we are good at and do well.

One of the first music learning experiences I remember was listening to music in preparation for a dancing act when I was in first grade. I was going to a neighborhood birthday party with my older sister, and they were playing rock and roll, the twist, and a dance called mashed potatoes. I could dance, but I did not know that this music was revolutionary and part of a historical movement during the sixties. I watched the Beatles on *The Ed Sullivan Show*. I also saw a British pop singer by the name of Tom Jones, a famous Spanish singer named Raphael, and a famous Puerto Rican singer, composer, and mambo and big band leader by the name of Tito Rodriguez.

I also listened to a rock and roll show at nights on WKVM radio in San Juan. I learned about Three Dog Night; Blood, Sweat and Tears; Chicago; Jimi Hendrix; Janis Joplin; Santana; and many other young musicians and bands of that era.

During eleventh grade at Francisco Zayas Santana High School, some of my friends decided they were going to put together a rock and roll band. They invited me to join the Dreamers. I decided I was going to play the bass. I asked my father to buy me an electric bass and a bass amplifier, and he did. My friend was the lead guitar player, and he was very good since he grew up in a family of musicians. I did not. I had never played a musical instrument, but I was amazed about how fast I was able to pick it up. I could hear the bass on the records I had, and I imagined myself doing the same thing. A Canadian rock and roll group influenced me tremendously because their recordings had strong bass sounds, and I loved it. I wanted to sound the same.

In twelfth grade, I was the bass player of a fifteen-piece big band group under the direction of a master musical director: a great music teacher at Inter-American University of Puerto Rico. He was a trumpet player and musical director of the Happy Hills Orchestra, a swinging big band of the seventies on the Island Music scene. We were impacted significantly by the Fania Records Salsa explosion taking place in New York City during the late sixties and early seventies. Motown Records in Detroit was expanding the musical universe by promoting great music written and performed by great African American artists. Fania Records was in New York City, promoting Latin music and making it available to the world. I did not know at the time that I had discovered one of my gifts: the gift of music.

We all have gifts. These are things that make us passionate. Many people have several gifts. This does not mean that we wake up one day and start doing this one thing in an extraordinary way. Maybe some people are able to do it in a short time, but the development of our gifts requires time and effort and lots of practice. It is like a weightlifter who works to develop their muscles or a basketball player who develops techniques with lots of practice over a long period of time. It takes time, effort, and pain to develop our gifts.

I learned over time that in order to define my purpose in life, I had to discover my gifts so I could use them to fulfill my purpose. In other words, discovering my gifts proved to be helpful and essential for finding my purpose.

When I completed my active duty commitment with the US Army, I moved to the great city of Chicago. I was blessed with the opportunity to work for a great institution: The First National Bank of Chicago, First Chicago Corporation. While I was going to college to complete my bachelor's degree in business, I worked tirelessly for First Chicago. I was part of a wave toward the modernization of banking, which involved large computers, small- and medium-sized computers, and software from IBM, Microsoft, Tandem, Directions, Digital Equipment Corporation, and others. I was promoted eleven times over a period of years. I learned about management and leadership from great mentors and teachers at First Chicago, Northeastern Illinois University, and Governors State University in Illinois. However, one of my most important discoveries during my young executive career was the understating that I was "good with people." I eventually understood emotionally and intellectually that I had the ability to relate to others in a positive way. I had great interpersonal skills. I had the ability to communicate effectively, and people liked working on my team. I discovered the gift of leading and helping others and the organization by bringing people together toward the achievement of extraordinary goals and objectives.

What can we do or be in life that will fulfill our purpose? We have many choices where we can serve humankind and plant seeds we can harvest as we grow and move on in life's continuously moving timeline. Life really is a journey through time and space, and it is critically important to define who we are and what we want to become in order to reach self-fulfillment. We can develop our potential and achieve self-fulfillment to be the best we can be in many ways:

Firemen. Great public servants who place their lives on the line every day to save lives and property.

Store workers, managers, and clerks. They are the tail end of commerce's supply chain and serve the consumer face-to-face in challenging circumstances that many people do not realize. Doing the impossible with the least amount of resources possible. My grandfather on my father's side owned a store. He was committed to serving people with extraordinary attention and care. I learned from him how to be courteous and respectful and how to listen and be prompt in attending to people's needs. When people buy something from you, they are buying the product or service and the way the transaction takes place. This is fundamental for ensuring they come back to you. It brings success to the business and great satisfaction to those delivering the transaction and developing that very important long-term relationship. It is about developing and managing that customer relationship and making people your customers for life. There is great joy in this endeavor.

Teachers. They have a great responsibility to pass on knowledge to the next generation. They have a huge burden on their shoulders. Our society does not do justice to this noble chosen path. Great teachers do it for the love and the joy of witnessing the new harvest grow bigger, stronger, and wiser, which translates into hope for the future. My grandfather was a teacher, the first in my hometown. My mother was a great teacher, and I have various aunts and uncles who became teachers and left a mark on young people.

Nurses. My Auntie Ruth and my sister Glenda were great nurses, and they were both very successful because they loved what they did every day, taking care of the sick and delivering babies, myself included. My auntie Air Force Major (retired) Ruth E. Gonzalez attended to the big event of delivering me when I was born. My sister Glenda is teacher of nurses at Inter-American University of Puerto Rico. She has worked as a nurse for the commonwealth's Government Health Department. This is what she does, and she does it well because she loves what she does.

Doctors. They make a commitment to learn about how our bodies and minds work in order to help us heal and live better lives. They are dedicated, hardworking individuals who invest in a long educational journey to help others extend their lives, and in this way, they become angels of the Lord.

Pilots. Whether it is military pilots or commercial pilots, these great individuals perform a risky but fascinating function in moving us through these flying machines that are heavier than air, yet they lift off the ground to take us from point A to point B. They protect and defend our interests and our way of life around the world with pride and passion.

Soldiers, Sailors, Airmen, and Marines. I am a soldier. One of my uncles was a soldier during World War II, and another one served in Korea with the US Army Sixty-Fifth Infantry, the *Borinqueneers*. Tears come to my eyes every time I think about my high school friends who died in Vietnam or all those who have given their lives to fight for our ideals in Iraq, Afghanistan, and other conflicts. I know great soldiers who had great successful military careers and have retired young enough to start a second career in private or public service. This is a career of honor, respect, and bravery. My auntie Ruth became a major with the US Air Force as a nurse. She dedicated more than twenty-five years of faithful service to the Air Force. When she retired in her forties, she went to work at a Veterans Administration Hospital for another twenty years. What a great example of a public servant. For her, it was not work to be a nurse. It was a joy because she was fulfilling her purpose in life.

Police Officers. When we study all the aspects of the universe, we find order. Even when situations seem chaotic, at the end, we see the order that it is necessary to coexist. Law and order is about helping keeping order in our society. It is about serving and protecting the public by keeping order.

Clergy. My auntie Anna was the faithful wife of a great Evangelical pastor who I admired. They were great examples of dedication, selfless life, faith beyond the imaginable, and miracles. I need to write another book to tell their inspiring story. I was blessed to share great moments with Father Eddie, a young priest of the Catholic diocese in Caguas, Puerto Rico. He was a spiritual young man who inspired many and lived for his chosen path in life: to serve others.

Accountants. We need to keep track of the many gifts we receive and are responsible for. This is about recording all of life's transactions so we can respond to others for our stewardship. It is about learning from what we have recorded as the life of our institutions moves forward every day and using this information to plan for the future in business, on public service, at home, and everywhere else. One of my uncles was a certified public accountant, and he had a great career of dedicated service. My beautiful stepdaughter Jessica became a certified public accountant at a very young age. She serves proudly in the public service and has a long and prosperous career ahead of her.

Attorney. My uncle Uriel Zayas was an attorney, and his son, Uriel Jr., is an attorney as well. I will always be proud of them. In our society, we need responsible individuals who can sort through our legal system and be intermediaries in all aspects of life. This is what they do, and this is how they serve others.

- Finding My Purpose, Finding My Way in Life -

Engineers. I have two cousins who are engineers. One lives in New York City, and the other one lives in California. They followed their hearts and have accomplished great things in their careers by helping humanity solve problems that are important to our society. I also have some friends who graduated from engineering schools and went on to have great careers.

Actors. I acted in plays when I was child. However, it was not my calling. I never felt a strong desire to follow that path. I admire great actors who have rendered tremendous performances and earned prominent places in our lives, in our hearts, and in the universe: Marlon Brando, Al Pacino, Sidney Poitier, Robert De Niro, Jose Ferrer, Jack Nicholson, Samuel Jackson, Benicio del Toro, Zoe Saldaña, Harrison Ford, Raul Julia, Denzel Washington, Jennifer Lawrence, Julia Roberts, Noomi Rapace, Matt Damon, Matthew McConaughey, and many others.

Singers and Musicians. This is a most passionate path for me. I love music and have played musical instruments since I was young. However, early in my life, I received a clear message from people who were important in my life: "A musician? Forget it! You will die of starvation and will never amount to anything!"

Is this statement true? Definitively not. Absolutely not! However, negative feedback can be very destructive to the human mind. If we allow it, negative feedback can be planted in our minds and can grow to become a strong belief—even if it is not true. I know many musicians and singers who have made a living and dedicated their lives to their musical passions. In the process, they made substantial contributions to our society with the gifts the Lord has given them. I can talk about John Birks, Dizzy Gillespie, Stevie Wonder, Mongo Santamaria, Herbie Hancock, Tito Puente, Eddie Palmieri, La Sonora Ponceña, and Poncho Sanchez and his Latin Jazz Band, among many, many great individuals who passionately dedicated their lives to music. I have come to know these people at a very personal level. I can tell you about their struggles and perseverance to overcome many obstacles. What about Esperanza Spalding? What a great story of dedication and passion for your gifts. The important thing is to follow your gifts and passions, and you will achieve a level of performance where you will be respected and command a decent living at the very least. It is possible. Mark 9:23 says, "Jesus said unto him, If thou can believe, all things are possible to him that believeth."

Politicians. We are blessed with being part of the greatest democracy in the world today. We do not have a perfect democracy, but it is a work in progress—and it requires the collaboration of all of us. We need individuals in our society to dedicate their lives to serve others through public service in elected positions and otherwise. We need strong leadership and people with convictions and values who know who we are as a people: "We the people" "and justice for all." We need people with solid values and moral, ethical principles to serve at local, state, and federal levels. This path, like all others, requires a lot of hard work, dedication, and perseverance. It always has. Do you know how many times President Lincoln failed while running for public office? What a legacy he left for us. And in this way, many other great individuals have contributed greatly to our nation by choosing the path of politics.

Housewives. This is a very honorable path, like all the other examples. This requires a great self-sacrifice for the benefit of youngsters who must be educated and cared for. Being a mother, a wife, and household chief executive officer is a great honor. It requires our admiration and our support. Titles are meant to describe what people do and who they are. However, the title of housewife historically has been misunderstood and unappreciated. It is time we come to understand it and respect those individuals who choose to follow this path in life.

Bankers. Our banking system provides a framework under which our financial system functions. It is a framework to exchange goods, services, and other resources to provide what our society needs. In the same way the goods flow from raw materials, through a supply chain management process until the end, at the consumer's hand, the financial resources move with the same flow. Our governments at all levels move resources around, and as part of this network, they provide services that keep our society in order. It is a fascinating story, and it is a fascinating system that is built on trust. I was a banker for a while during my young professional years. This experience was an honor and a blessing from the Lord. He wanted me to experience this world so I could share these experiences with others.

Logisticians. Today, I am a logistician. According to the US Department of Labor, "Logisticians analyze and coordinate an organization's supply chain—the system that moves a product from supplier to consumer. They manage the entire life cycle of a product, which includes how a product is acquired, distributed, allocated, and delivered." This means we get involved in the entire process of taking a product or service from an idea, concept, or plan to raw materials, manufacturing, and distribution all the way to the consumer and its return if there are problems with the product or service. This is a very fascinating field, and according to the US Labor Department, it promises to have a 22 percent increase in opportunities in 2022.

Social Workers. I have a very dear friend in my beloved city of Chicago who has worked for the state of Illinois Department of Social Services for more than thirty years. She says that she has no plans for retirement. She feels joy in helping people deal with family problems, unemployment, alcoholism, drug addiction, and many other social issues that are usually concentrated on the lower scales of our society, but not exclusively. She is engaged in this crusade in the City of Big Shoulders: Chicago, Illinois. This is her calling. She is the face of God for many people in need.

Hospitality Workers. My two daughters have chosen the hospitality industry as their way to earn a living while serving others. Each one is unique and has its own gifts. However, both are passionate about serving people face-to-face while they are trying to be a home away from home. They worked for a great hotel chain with an internationally renowned name. They worked in a historic hotel in Chicago and in a beautiful property in Ponce, Puerto Rico. One has been named supervisor of the year on various occasions, and the other one earned employee of the year at one of Chicago's biggest and most prestigious hotels. She also was promoted recently. Why have they earned this recognition? Because they are passionate about what they do. They enjoy what they do, which is serving guests and making them feel special. It takes some very special skills to work with people and deal with them on a foundation of respect, trust, consideration, and mutual understanding. This is a special gift from the Lord. I see them going all the way to the top in their careers and chosen profession.

Auto Technicians. My father loved cars. He learned to do auto body work and paint cars at an early age. He went on to be the service supervisor at Ford's Southern Auto Sales. From there, he went on to have his own successful auto body and auto service business: Recondition Auto Shop, Inc. I worked with my father every time I had an opportunity during my school vacations, and he paid me well—just like he paid all his employees. I learned to love automobiles, appreciate their utility, and understand how they function. This can be a very profitable path, but like all others, it requires perseverance, hard work, dedication, and a commitment to be better than the competition while serving people beyond their expectations. My father was respected for his commitment to quality and service. Because of his dedication, he achieved great success in his chosen path in life. His goal was to give people more than what they paid for and amaze his customers.

Carpenters, Masons, and Construction Workers. Jesus was the son of a carpenter. His earthly father was a carpenter: Joseph. Today, construction of housing and buildings in general involves many different trades and professions: plumbers, masons, carpenters, electricians, engineers, architects. The list is long. It represents a great field of opportunities. I worked with individuals who have done great work in this field because they love what they do. I have known others who are a disaster because they feel they are obligated to do this work because they do not have another choice. That is simply not true. I was involved in construction by rehabilitating various old buildings in Chicago. I also built various residential properties. They were challenging and uplifting experiences.

Entrepreneurs. Steve Jobs is probably one the best example of what entrepreneurs do and why they do what they do. I have various books that present several aspects of his life. However, I personally followed the rise and fall of Steve Jobs and Steve Wozniak as they started Apple Computers in 1976. Steve Jobs had a vision, maybe blurry at times, but it was an incredible vision to have personal computers as a home appliance like a stove, refrigerator, or television set. That vision is now real. I owned an Apple IIe, an Apple IIc, and one of the early Macs in 1986. I purchased two eMacs, the education version of the early iMacs. I own various iPhones and iPads. My music library, iTunes, has thousands of songs. I purchased these products because I found them to be of good quality and useful in helping me live a better life and manage my affairs more efficiently. I also used many other brands of Intel/Windows-based products, but Apple's quality and utility are unsurpassed. The results are clear. All these Apple products were not the result of Steve Jobs's efforts alone. It took the effort of many, many people to make this happen over a long period of time. However, Steve had one of the most important qualities of a great leader: they inspire a shared vision. They "have visions and dreams of what could be and are able to communicate them to others" (*The Five Practices of Exemplary Leadership*, Kouzes, J. M and Posner, B. Z. 2007).

These are some of the ways to serve that come to mind. There are many other ways to serve well and earn a living in the world today. I am sure there are many other professions, trades, and constructive and positive manners on which we can serve others, make a living, and support our families and our communities. Whatever it is, we will do well and accomplish extraordinary things when we love what it is we do.

David C. Novak became executive chairman of Yum! Brands on January 1, 2015. Yum! Brands is Kentucky Fried Chicken, Pizza Hut, Taco Bell, Yum China, and Yum India.

In an interview published in the *New York Times* in 2009, he said the following about individuals in business who have extraordinary leadership skills:

> Gifts, as is the gift of music, or public speaking, or teaching ...They soak up everything they can possibly soak up so that they can become the best possible leader they can be. And then they share that with others. I don't know where I developed that trait, but I've had the good fortune of loving what I do since the minute I got into business. And because I can't get enough of it, I want to keep learning about it.

"Soaking up" is absorbing and learning to be better, to be the best that we can be. He says he had the fortune of loving what he does; therefore, he devotes himself to his chosen profession, heart and soul, and does extraordinarily well. According to the latest information on the Yum! Brands website, Mr. Novak is executive chairman:

> During his tenure as CEO since 1999, Yum! Brands doubled in size to 41,000 restaurants and established itself as a global powerhouse going from

Finding My Purpose, Finding My Way in Life

approximately 20 percent of its profits coming from outside the United States in 1997 to nearly 70 percent in 2013, while remaining an industry leader in return on invested capital.

When you love what you do, you tend to get the shots you throw to the basket in, like Michael Jordan did, and earn recognition. However, most importantly, we get personal satisfaction with an outstanding performance, which contributes to the team's winning.

Steve Jobs described this matter of finding our purpose and clearly identifying what we love to do when he addressed a graduating class at Stanford University in 2005:

> You've got to find what you love. And that is as true for your work as it is for your lovers. Your work is going to fill a large part of your life, and the only way to be truly satisfied is to do what you believe is great work. And the only way to do great work is to love what you do. If you haven't found it yet, keep looking. Don't settle. As with all matters of the heart, you'll know when you find it.

In all ways, the end result that we seek is the discovery of a chosen way to earn a living and fulfill our purpose in life. We are looking for a way to serve others in a way that helps others benefit in an extraordinary way. We want others to find completeness and help them live better and achieve their dreams and goals.

Those of us who have found a way to serve others with joy have also found fulfillment.

Image of red flower tree and a way ahead road

Oh my Lord, as thy soul liveth, my Lord, I am the woman that stood by thee here, praying unto the Lord. For this child I prayed and the Lord hath given me my petition which I asked of him.
—1 Samuel 1:26–27

CHAPTER 3

Imagination, Dreams, and Aspirations

There is so much that can be said about the human mind, and we have limited knowledge, time, and space to address it all. I am not a psychologist or psychiatrist; therefore, what I can say about the science behind the human mind is limited. However, I can tell you a lot about this subject based on my own personal experiences, the experiences of those whose lives I have witnessed, and the experiences of others through the readings I have done about this subject.

I know the ability to imagine things and develop a clear picture in our minds of what we would like to see happen in the future is a gift from the Creator. In other words, humans come "factory equipped" with this faculty. Some people develop it more than others. This is influenced by many factors. However, the most important factor that influences our faculty to use our minds to imagine things, dream, and aspire is the ability to believe.

Merriam-Webster defines believe as "to accept something as true, genuine, or real" (6). To imagine things is to "see" things in our minds that are not yet real. Therefore, the element of "believing" is fundamental in order for us to be able to transform the abstract thoughts, dreams, and aspirations that we may be cultivating. We are unable to touch them; to be able to transform our thoughts, dreams, and aspirations into concrete and real things, we must believe that our dreams and aspirations can actually happen and believe we are deserving of such blessings.

This is not magic, hocus-pocus, or silly nonsense. There is a spiritual world, which we do not see with the eyes of the flesh. It is very real, and we are constantly battling the influences they have on us and those around us. Wherever there is doubt, fear, insecurity, discord, feelings of unworthiness, or similar destructive influences, we are confronting influences of the evil spiritual world. Many people dismiss this matter as old ladies' myths and witch stories, but the truth is that the battle is quite real. The good news is that we can win this spiritual war with the presence of the Holy Spirit in our lives. We can battle evil and conquer mountains in the name of our Lord Jesus Christ.

The act of believing is, like many other character traits, cultivated over time. It starts in early childhood. I have known individuals who do not even believe in electricity. This is just an expression, which means they do not believe in anything. It starts with the fact that they do not believe in their own worth as humans. Therefore, they are unable to believe that others can give them affection in any way. For the most part, it has to do with the fact that they have not experienced love in their lives.

When we experience love in our lives, our hearts and minds open up. We learn that love is the greatest force in the universe, which binds all things. God is love! All love forms and expressions come the Lord of lords, Creator of the entire universe. He who was, who is, and who will be into eternity. He says, I Am. He loves all things in His creation: humans, animals, plants, and many things we do not even know about yet.

Love opens the door for hope, and hope says, "Maybe; there are possibilities; things can happen." Hope gives us the ability to expect good things to happen. With hope, our attitudes change—and we can see colors better. We can see the yellows, the reds, the greens, and the blues more brilliantly. Hope leads to clear visions of what could be. And when the vision becomes clear in our minds, when it takes shape to the point that we can see the colors, smell, touch, feel, hear, and sense what we want to realize, it leads to enthusiasm.

Dr. Norman Vincent Peale's *Enthusiasm Makes the Difference* says that enthusiasm is an emotion that is a result of the anticipation of things to come. In other words, as we dream and imagine that which we believe can be, anticipation builds as a result of the picture we develop in our minds and hearts of the possibilities of realizing this dream or idea we really want to come to pass.

We can shape our dreams and aspirations and clearly formulate what can be and what we would like to happen in the future—all of it, in our minds—before it actually happens. We refer to this faculty as using the gift of imagination.

Of the many gifts received from our Lord, the ability to use our minds and project the future, in our minds, before things actually happen, is called imagination. We have the ability to develop our imagination and use this skill, this gift, to help us transform dreams and ideas into those things we want to become real in our lives.

Imagination is about looking down the path, to the future, and being able to articulate what we see with our minds—and then turning those images into very specific expressions of what we see and what we want the future to be.

We also need to comprehend that our words have power, especially what we say to ourselves. The words we plant in our minds will bring about good things if they are the right words. This ongoing conversation with ourselves is a very important aspect of our lives, and it influences our imaginations greatly. We have the ability to learn, and through positive self-talk, we can influence our thinking and improve our mindsets in order to face the challenges we face every day. Life is a lot about preparing for the opportunities that we know we will find. Plan and prepare for the opportunities that will come:

> For as the rain cometh down, and the snow from heaven, and returneth not thither, but watereth the

earth, and maketh it bring forth and bud, that it may give seed to the sower, and bread to the eater: So shall my word be that goeth forth out of my mouth: it shall not return unto me void, but it shall accomplish that which I please, and it shall prosper in the thing whereto I sent it. (Isaiah 55:10–11)

The words we think about and speak have power, and they will become real in our lives. All the information and images that come to our minds—through all our senses—work toward creating the reality that becomes who we are. The ideas develop into the words we think, speak, and act on.

We transform these ideas into words, which trigger actions as we repeat them and focus all our energy on them. Therefore, we need to speak constructive words that lead to positive and affirmative steps to move us toward the realization of what we are searching for in life. Amen.

Our founding fathers had a dream that all people here at the time and those yet to come would enjoy freedom and prosperity. They imagined equality and wrote this dream in the Declaration of Independence. Is the dream fulfilled? Not 100 percent. However, we have progressed so much, and we continue to work as a nation to make this dream real. All of this is true because transforming dreams into reality is a process.

When we have a small dream, the process requires effort, planning, and perseverance to see it through until it becomes real before our eyes. It is always like this. Transforming our dreams, goals, and aspirations is a process that starts with thoughts and ideas.

When we have big dreams, the process requires a big effort. With big or small dreams, we must understand that we have the faculty of transforming our thoughts and dreams into reality. First, we have to come to the realization that when we have a good idea—a dream that burns inside our hearts and minds—it is not an accident. God's will for our lives is manifested through His Word, through people and angels, messengers that reveal things to us and the circumstances we live in.

When we have a good idea, a good dream in our minds and in our hearts, it comes from the Lord. God is love. The things, thoughts, ideas, and dreams He places in our hearts and minds, He means for us to fulfill them. Therefore, He will provide whatever guidance and resources we need to make it happen. All of this for His glory. All of this because His love is beyond our understanding.

If our ideas are negative, evil, destructive, or selfish, they are not from the Lord—and things will not go well if we follow their path.

When I was a child, we lived not too far from Ramey Air Force Base. At the time, there was a squadron of Boeing B-52 strategic bombers at Ramey. This aircraft is very noisy. It has eight jet engines, and I could hear them coming from far away as they were making their landing approach. I would stay quietly, listening to the aircraft coming, but not actually seeing them until they came over the mountains and into Ramey's landing strips. These were great experiences for me as a child and influenced me tremendously—as much as the yellow biplane that used to irrigate the sugarcane fields when I was in first grade. To this day, Boeing B-52s are still in service in the United States Air Force.

As the B-52 has endured as a viable aircraft for our beloved air force for so many years, the memories have endured in my mind and my heart. I own a collection of more than 350 die-cast military aircrafts, which I cherish very much. I have collected these models over the course of many years.

As a child, I had dreams of flying aircraft, which were influenced by those early experiences. I was so passionate. I learned the different model names, numbers, and manufacturers of commercial and military aircraft. I asked my parents for a pilot outfit for Christmas, and I got that present. I remember being delighted with that pilot suit and all my toy aircraft. But what happened to the dream?

I know what happened to my early childhood dream. The transformation of dreams, goals, and aspirations does not happen overnight. There is a process we must follow. The dream, thought, goal, or idea is a seed. When we plant seeds, they must be cultivated with dedication. Once the seeds are planted, we must tend to them and care for them—the same as when we plant corn or pea seeds, as my grandmother taught me. Once planted, seeds must receive love, attention, and all the care and resources like water that are necessary for the seed to germinate, grow, and produce fruit.

During my early childhood, we lived in a small farm with pigs, chickens, goats, rabbits, plantains, a small corn field, and pigeon peas. When my grandmother was planting pigeon peas, I told her I wanted to help. Who can say no to a small child they love? She showed me how to make a small opening in the soft ground, which was already plowed, and then place three seeds in the hole and cover it. Then we moved to dig the next opening a reasonable distance apart. We did this until it got too hot, and then we went back to the house for lunch and to refresh.

The next morning, I went to the field to see what was happening with the seeds we had planted. I was opening up the holes we had dug for the seeds.

It did not take long for my grandmother to yell to me to stop and leave the field alone. She was not happy. She got me out of the field quickly and asked, "What are you doing?"

I told her I wanted to see what was happening with the seeds. I asked where the plant was that she was taking about.

She sat me down and slowly explained that it required time for the plants to grow. They required care, water, love, and time. She was right because she had seen this process time and time again. In a few weeks, we could see the little plants coming out of the ground. Then the pigeon plants started growing. It took many months. However, as the Christmas season was almost upon us, the fruits of the pigeon peas were ready to be harvested. I also participated in the efforts of collecting the harvest and processing the peas. Nevertheless, it was not until many years later that I really understood the depth of that lesson.

Thoughts are things—and peas seeds are things. Both can be planted and with time, they can produce a harvest.

It all starts with a thought. Grab the thought. Write it down. Describe your dream fully with the details you are able to see in your mind. Then start the process of researching your dream: Who has written about it? Who is living this dream? How did they get there? What resources are required? Who can you talk to about this one thing you want to realize in your life? Get information about how you can start working on making your dream a reality. This is very important. We will never have all the information required to start. If we wait until everything is 100 percent perfect to get started, we may never get started. Therefore, we have to get started.

With the information we gather, we must develop a plan. A plan is but a projection of what we want things to be in the future—like a sales and inventory forecast or a weather forecast. We must be prepared to adjust our plans as we move forward because situations change, storms take different directions, and our customers are going to change their minds. Life is constantly changing, and we must be aware of this fact and regularly review where we are, according to plan, and where we really want to go.

It is a process, and we are going to need assistance from others. Therefore, it is important to seek advice and be humble about the fact that we do not know everything. It is good to get feedback:

> Without counsel purposes are disappointed, but in the multitude of counselors they are established.
> (Proverbs 15:22)

We want also to be firm on our convictions and clear about what we are in the process of accomplishing. Why do we want to accomplish our dreams? We need to answer this question for ourselves. No one can answer this question for us. However, consulting other people we have come to respect is very important.

Consult others —seek advice from mentors, elders, and others who have already gone through this road. This consultation can take shape in many different ways. One way is to read what others have written about what we want to accomplish and why. Read books on the subject, seek spiritual guidance, and place the plan in the Lord's hands. That is the most important guidance we can ever obtain. The Lord is with us, and He listens and answers. Humble yourself, go before him, and get your mind ready to receive wisdom from above.

It's time to execute the plan and take action. As we move forward, we will find obstacles. Some challenges we knew would be there from the research we have done, and some challenges we did not know would be there. Nevertheless, we have to keep a positive attitude to overcome the obstacles we find. We must face them with courage and develop a clear image of who we are, what we are working toward, and why we want to accomplish this goal, dream, or aspiration.

Why do we want to climb this mountain? Who makes up the team of people who are helping me achieve the dreams in my life? Keep a positive attitude. Everything is possible. In *Attitude Is Everything*, Keith Harrell wrote, "Attitude is everything because it is involved in everything. It impacts our performance at work, (in school), our relationships. Attitude is the cornerstone upon which we build our lives." He says that attitude is a state of mind that will affect everything we do in life.

In, *Mindset: The New Psychology of Success*, Dr. Carol S. Dweck (10) describes mindset as the beliefs that determine whether we develop our full potential or remain stagnant in life. According to Dr. Dweck, there are only two types of mindsets: *fixed mindset* or *growth mindset*. The fixed mindset believes life is overcome by circumstances, and it surrenders. The growth mindset develops because we learn to believe in the development of human potential. It helps us build strong character. Character grows from our mindsets. When we open our minds to the possibilities of what can be accomplished, we learn to develop empathy with others, we develop a big heart to help others along the way because we have learned that things are possible, and we have a responsibility to share with others in order to help them grow. Most importantly, a growth mindset helps us with our character to make it through the difficulties, be strong, and face failure and obstacles.

If at first we do not succeed, we need to get up and try again—and try again and again and again until we accomplish what we set out to do.

In life, there are times when we suffer setbacks. When this happens, we need to get through the initial emotions of failure and disappointment as quickly as possible and get back to work on improving our plan. We need to take action again. It is hard work, but when we stay focused on the end result, we will continue until we say, "This is the day I realized my dream, my goal, and my aspirations!" It is going to happen when we stay with it.

Let's enjoy the road to the realization of our dreams! Let's also share our successes, which are blessings and gifts from the Almighty, with others.

Butterflies by the Lake Churchill

And God saw every thing that he had made, and, behold, it was very good. And the evening and the morning were the sixth day.
—Genesis 1:31

CHAPTER 4

Organized Planning

During my retail management career, which covers several decades, we had a market executive / market leader who we all referred to as "Darth Vader." He was tall, had a strong and deep voice, and possessed an intimidating and commanding presence. In addition, he had a very successful career in retail management for many years. When he spoke, people listened to him.

Many things can be said about his legacy, but his biggest impact on my career was during a meeting we had in San Juan. The subject of the meeting was something I knew about because I had studied it and practiced it, but it was like a cover over my eyes was lifted.

He asked, "What does it takes to be a successful big box retail store manager?"

The room was completely silent.

He stood there and looked at us for a very long time.

No one dared to address him or even try to answer that question. What he said shocked everyone because it was very simple. We were expecting a complicated formula, but his answer was not a big secret. We were all familiar with the idea and concept.

He said, "To be a successful big box retail store manager, you have to be prepared. To be prepared, you have to develop the habit of having organized plans. Not a one-time organized plan for an executive visit to impress your superiors, but an organized plan for the everyday execution of your strategy."

His answer has many angles we can look at and analyze, but the main message is that accomplishing anything in life requires preparation, and preparation requires planning. In addition, we need to make the habit of planning every day, for the next thirty days, for the next ninety days, for the next 365 days, and so on.

It is important to make clear that planning is a process that is constantly evolving. Our plans must be constantly reviewed and updated. Planning is looking at the future, and we do not know exactly what the future is going to be like. Only God Almighty knows what exactly the future is going to be. However, based on the dreams, goals, and aspirations we have, the research we require, and the rest of the available information, we can develop plans that can guide us toward the realization of what we aspire to do or be.

I first realized the importance of organized planning while reading *Think and Grow Rich*. Napoleon Hill published the first edition in 1937.

> The most intelligent man living cannot succeed in ... any undertaking ... without plans that are practical and workable. Just keep in mind and remember when your plan fails, that temporary defeat is not permanent failure. It may only mean that your plans have not been sound. Build another plan. Start all over again. (11)

> No individual has sufficient experience, education, natural abilities and knowledge to insure ... (realization of his or her plans) ... without the cooperation of other people. (11)

We must develop plans that are practical and workable, and in the process of developing those plans, we must solicit and obtain

- Finding My Purpose, Finding My Way in Life -

the cooperation of other people. We have to understand that we do not know everything that there is to know. We will never know everything there is to know about any subject in particular. Not even individuals with very high degrees of skills and education—subject matter experts—know everything about their fields. Scientists, engineers, musicians, and many other experts constantly seek collaboration in their endeavors. This is a critical aspect of planning: the need for collaboration during the development of our plans and the execution of our plans.

Whether we are middle school students, high school students, college students working on a business major, accounting, chemistry, or a medical doctorate, teachers, engineers, or automotive transmissions specialists, developing a plan will go a long way toward achieving our goals. When we want to become a professional in a chosen field, in order to excel, it requires effort, focus, and practice, practice, practice. All these things come together more effectively when we are following a definite plan to achieve or become something.

This is true whether we are seeking an education to obtain a required license, a professional certificate, or a diploma to be able to earn our living on a particular field, working toward becoming an entrepreneur, or becoming a professional musician or athlete.

There are many references on how to develop a plan that is practical and workable. However, Zig Ziglar defined the process best in *Goals* (11).

The first step in the development of any plan, to achieve any goal, dream, or aspiration is that we must clearly identify and define exactly what we want to accomplish. The emphasis is on clearly defining exactly what we want to accomplish. This is critical because completing this part of the process will impact the entire plan's development. In this first step of the planning process, it is critical that we follow this instruction and write down the goal, desire, or aspiration. This writing must include details such as color, smell, taste, touch, sound, and the feeling of joy. In other words, it involves using our God-given gift of imagination and being able to develop a picture on our minds, which includes all our senses, and then taking the first step of transforming the abstract thought or idea into a concrete reality. The first step in this process is to write down the idea we have in our mind with all its details. It may take a few tries to get our idea, dream, or aspiration written down as we see it in our minds. This means identifying which mountain we are going to climb, how tall this mountain is, when we plan to climb it, and what we are going to do when get to the top.

The second step on the development of our plan is that we must define exactly why we want to accomplish the goal. This means clearly describing why this goal is important to us. For example, in my case, the primary reason I wanted to write this book was to leave it as a legacy for my grandchildren. This reason is emotional. It means, I have done it for the love I have for my daughters and grandsons and granddaughter. This is a powerful reason for doing anything in life. The reason we do whatever we do will move us forward and will help us refuel our souls with energy in order to overcome the obstacles that we must in order to conquer our goals, dreams, and aspirations.

The third step is to identify what obstacles I have to overcome to accomplish these goals. It is essential that we study what is required to obtain what we aspire to achieve our goals. It is necessary that we perform the necessary research on what is required to attain our goals. When do this, we will find out what obstacles and requirements we must fulfill during the journey toward accomplishing of our goals. For example, in a career development plan for the federal government, we discover that to be considered for an executive position as grade general services level 15, a certain type of business degree or experience is required. If we do not hold that degree or have that experience, the requirements are obstacles to attaining that goal.

Once we identify the real and potential obstacles, we need to develop a plan to overcome the obstacles. We need to get the degree or the necessary experience. We may need to obtain additional resources, or accomplishing our goal will take additional time. However, we should focus on the positive, which is that when we identify the real or potential obstacles, we are closer to the accomplishment of our goals because we have new information that gives us power over our circumstances to transform our dreams, ideas, goals, and aspirations into concrete things. Napoleon Hill said, "Knowledge is power." I know this is true.

The fourth step is that we must identify which people we need to reach out to in order to accomplish these goals. We need to identify the people we may need support from in some fashion because it is always the case that we'll need support. We will always need the help of others in various capacities and at various levels. We are individually responsible for the development of skills and talents and developing our will and character to attain our purpose in life.

We may not have all the knowledge or resources required to achieve our goals. However, others may have something we need to know or a resource we may require. In order to achieve our goals, we need to be able to work with others. In the process of accomplishing our goals, we need to request the assistance of others in exchange for helping them accomplish their goals.

There is a need for a constant exchange of ideas and resources and helping others on the journey toward what we want to accomplish in life. Mount Everest is literally located at the top of the world, rising 29,035 feet (8,850 meters) above sea level. We need a team of many individuals to help us reach the top. We need to obtain knowledge about a great deal of subjects, and we need guidance and direction. Even the most experienced mountain climbers require the help of a team. Therefore, we need to establish a positive relationship with individuals who may give us counsel and support.

The fifth step is that we must identify specifically which things we need to know to accomplish these goals. What do I need to know about the circumstances and details that make up the subject on my desire, goal, or objective? If my goal is to be an air force pilot, I have to find out which avenues I may be able to follow to get there. If I want to be a lawyer, I need to know which schools I may need to attend, how much it is going to cost, and what specialty within the profession I may be able to serve well based on my skills? Many questions need to be answered. What resources are required? What obstacles am I likely to face?

Therefore, we must research the subject. Obtain knowledge about my goals, dreams, and aspirations. As we acquire knowledge about the subject we are studying, we acquire understanding of how to overcome obstacles and obtain what we seek. If I pursue a career path that requires a certain degree or type of experience, then I have to decide how to overcome these obstacles.

The sixth step is that we must define specific action steps that will get the plan in motion and moving forward toward its realization. A detailed plan is always necessary. When commercial pilots develop and file their flight plans, they establish the path they will follow to get from their current location to their planned destination. In these flight plans, commercial pilots identify the navigation points they plan to follow on their way to their destination. They will follow this plan and take steps to stay in the course originally planned by taking steps to follow those navigation points. Sometimes they have to alter their plans because of circumstances they did not anticipate, like a weather system. In the same manner, we must identify the required action steps to move toward the realization of our goals and the arrival at our destination.

This is also a very critical step because we must have a workable plan that is based on the facts and knowledge we have gained. There is no such thing as a perfect plan. Plans can always be improved. We cannot wait forever for the perfect plan, but we must make an effort to have the best information available with the resources we have at our disposal—and then take action.

The steps must lead to the development of a detailed plan. We must take action and keep them in motion until our goals are achieved.

- Finding My Purpose, Finding My Way in Life -

The seventh step is to define and determine a specific date—month, day, and year—when we expect to complete the execution of the plan and accomplish this goal.

Once we clearly define our goal or destination, we must define a specific date when the goal is to be attained. The date must come from the knowledge and understating we have acquired while doing research about what we want to accomplish.

This plan must be written and must contain all the necessary information to keep us on track. We can use a simple spreadsheet to develop our plan: the what, the when, the resources required, and when we plan to achieve it.

It is critically important to understand that when we develop a plan, it is not the end of the planning process. Planning is an ongoing process. It constantly evolves as circumstances evolve on our way to the achievement of our goals.

Plans will fail. Therefore, we must be prepared, get up when fall, and build another plan. When we fail, we have additional information we can use to improve our plan and start again. We have to rework our plan and start again. This will help us to develop perseverance, which means to continue on in spite of obstacles and circumstances. This will strengthen character and move us toward the realization of our goals, dreams, and aspirations.

The eighth step is to see myself already in possession of the goal I have set. This is the gift of imagination. This is about painting a picture in our minds and hearts as already achieving what we desire to accomplish. The writing and development of our plan will help us use our imaginations to visualize what we are pursuing. Pictures and photographs will also help us nurture our dreams, goals, and aspirations and attain what we seek.

There are many ways to develop our visualization skills. I have developed a habit of practicing or acting as if I have already achieved my goal. Early in my management career, I aspired to be an operations supervisor of the great institution I was working at. The position was occupied by my mentor. He was a great man. I started taking notes about the things he did, including how he answered the phone and how he dealt with issues and solved problems. He was a dynamic individual. I started acting like him. I used to practice at home how to react and engage people in the process of getting things done.

This institution handled billions of dollars, and my mentor was very effective in supporting all the people involved in this business: employees, customers, and management. I learned from my mentor, and I saw myself as being on his position. I developed a plan, and I worked hard to earn the trust of the organization. Therefore, I achieved my goals. Among all the elements required for the achievement of this goal, visualization was very important. Practicing the required skills was very influential in strengthening my skills, improving my attitude, and developing my confidence. Eventually, I was promoted to the position of my mentor because I saw myself doing this job. I was inspired to make the effort to learn, and I performed as required to earn this position.

The ninth step is execution of the plan. Execution of the plan means transforming our attitudes into actions. We have to learn to believe, plan in detail what we want to accomplish, execute the plan, and do the things we planned to do. This is the third step in the transformation of dreams, goals, and aspirations into real things on our lives. We need to work hard and stay focused. We must have a written plan that we have researched and prepared with diligence. We must constantly review and improve the plan. Execution is about bringing it all together.

The first step is the idea in our hearts and minds, the second step is to write it down into a plan, and the third step is take action to transform the abstract into the concrete—into the real world—and make our goals, dreams, and aspirations real. It is critically important that we move forward with confidence.

Our attitude will help us develop confidence. As John C. Maxwell wrote in *The Difference Maker*, "Attitude is the difference maker —it brings about confidence." We can look at life and focus on what can be by moving forward with confidence. In addition, as we develop our skills, it brings about competence, which brings about confidence. Experience gives us knowledge, which results in competence, which brings more confidence.

A good and positive attitude can help us develop the confidence required to do the things we aspire to in life. A good positive attitude will help us develop into the great person we can be in order to achieve extraordinary things. A good positive attitude will help us develop the necessary skills to achieve a high level of performance, which will lead to competence and confidence.

As we review and measure our progress, we will better understand how we are doing and see how we can make corrections and improvements. This will help us develop confidence and move us through to the execution of the plan and the realization of our goals. We need to update our plans as needed and stay with them until our goals are accomplished.

I would like to add the following planning steps:

- See myself as worthy, capable, and already in possession of the goals I have decided to reach for and for which I am committed to work hard to attain.
- Place my plans before God in prayer. Place my goals and the plan to accomplish them and ask for wisdom, courage, and strength to follow His will and fulfill my mission in life.
- Set up a binder where I can place each goal and my plans to accomplish each goal. Keep all my documents and update my plans in one location. This works great for me in terms of organization and following up. I review and update my goals regularly, daily, weekly, and set a schedule to do this. I record my progress in the binder. The color pictures in this binder demonstrate what my goal is.

The most important of all the steps we may take during the development of our plans—the transformation of our ideas into reality—is to go to our Lord in prayer and place our lives in His hands.

Read Psalm 37:4 and Psalm 1:1–5 regularly and meditate on your goals after reading them. The Lord promises that when we delight ourselves in him, He will grant us our desires. This is what the Word of God says:

> Delight thyself also in the Lord:, and he shall give thee the desires of thine heart. (Psalm 37:4)

I believe it and give testimony to the fact that the Lord listens and answers our prayers:

> Blessed is the man that walketh not in the counsel of the ungodly, nor standeth in the way of sinners, nor sitteth in the seat of the scornful. But his delight is in the law of the Lord; and in his law doth he meditate day and night. And he shall be like a tree planted by the rivers of water, that bringeth forth his fruit in his season; his leaf also shall not wither; and whatsoever he doeth shall prosper. (Psalm 1:1–3)

> But the diligent man makes good use of everything he finds. (Proverbs 12:27b)

> But the soul of the diligent shall be made fat (prosperous). (Proverbs 13:4b)

Mountain in the horizon

And Jesus answering saith unto them, Have faith in God. For verily I say unto you, That whosoever shall say unto this mountain, Be thou removed, and be thou cast into the sea; and shall not doubt in his heart, but shall believe that those things which he saith shall come to pass; he shall have whatsoever he saith. Therefore I say unto you, What things soever ye desire, when ye pray, believe that ye receive them, and ye shall have them.
—Mark 11:22–24

CHAPTER 5

Execution of the Plan

We are a wonderfully made creature of God, a beautiful person who has many talents and gifts. God has a purpose for our lives, and through prayer, we may seek His presence in our lives so we can receive wisdom and courage to do well and become everything we were created to do.

Life is difficult. There are plenty of dragons and other monsters along the roads of life. There are many things in life that we will not be able to solve on our own. We are going to need help in executing our plans in life and overcoming the dragons and the hyenas that we sometimes have to confront in order to overcome and move toward the realization of our goals and dreams.

Some time ago, I heard a story about the lion and the hyenas. It is really a story about life in the universe, the mistakes we make, the challenges, and the necessity of getting help from others. When we get help from others, we witness God's intervention.

Lions live in families. They distinguish themselves in many ways from the rest of the animal kingdom. One of the characteristics that make them different is that they are the only big cats that live in groups, which are called prides. Once they reach a certain level of maturity, the males leave the pride for various reasons. The males leave the pride and explore the world to perhaps someday lead their own family.

- Finding My Purpose, Finding My Way in Life -

A beautiful, strong, young but mature lion made a mistake while discovering the world around him. He stopped paying attention to his surroundings, perhaps distracted by little things in front of him. He crossed a stream and climbed to higher ground—only to find himself in the middle of a pack of hungry hyenas.

The lion is a very strong and ferocious animal, and it has the power to take on one hyena any day. The lion is much stronger and is born with an attitude that he can take on other animals and overcome them. The strong character of a lion has been used to describe humans' attitudes and their desire to overcome. Many sports teams use the name "lions" to define their characteristics of strength and courage.

However, in this case, this lion was faced with more than twenty hungry hyenas. They were highly motivated by their hunger and were making intimidating noises. Hyenas like to operate in packs. Naturally, they know about their strength in numbers. Therefore, the hyenas were confident they could overcome the beautiful lion. The hyenas quickly surrounded the lion, charged him, and bit at him.

The lion defended himself bravely and damaged some of the hyenas. This went on for some time. The hyenas kept charging, biting the lion, and retreating. They repeated this action over and over again. The lion was distressed, hurt, and tired, and he was not making any progress in repelling the huge pack of hyenas. The lion fell on the floor. It looked like the hyenas were closed to killing the beautiful lion. It seriously looked like the lion was done, and these were his last moments.

However, another lion heard the first lion growling and fighting for his life. The second lion was related to the first lion. Perhaps it was his brother. When the second lion came and charged the hyenas, the first lion got up and found the strength to continue the fight and face the pack of hungry hyenas.

In a matter of seconds, the situation changed. The presence and force of two strong and ferocious lions and their lion attitude pushed the hyenas away. In a few minutes, the pack of hyenas left the scene running. The pair of lions inflicted some serious damage on some of the hyenas, and they won the day.

At the end, both lions engaged in a playful game with each other. The first lion said, "Thank you. You saved my life." The first lion was wounded, but he was happy to have received the help that made the difference and gave him another day to live.

In reflecting about this story, I was able to relate to the first lion immediately. Like the first lion and all lions, I can say that God also gifted me with strength, courage, and other great qualities. However, I made many mistakes in life that led to challenges and problems—much like the pack of hyenas.

There are moments in life when it appears that the end is near. We do not see a way out, and it looks like all the hyenas (problems and challenges) will win the day. In those times, we must keep our faith and seek God's supernatural intervention.

I do not know whether God will send another lion to help—or send rain or lightning—or in which form His awesome power and love will be manifested. The only thing I know is that His hand will be extended to me and a way forward will be found. It does not matter how difficult the circumstances may look. Trust the Lord in all things.

We must have a clear picture of the good things we want to accomplish in life—and not of what we fear. Based on the foundation of our God-given talents, strength, and courage, we are called to elaborate specific plans.

For the realization of our goals and objectives in life, there is a formula:

Believe

It all starts with a thought or an idea. Believe that it is possible to achieve what we want to accomplish in life, and it will be so.

Plan

It continues with the effort to develop a map that we can follow, using our gifts, resources, and wisdom from the Lord. We need information to be able to develop a good plan—not a perfect plan, but a good plan. It is also important to understand that planning is a process. In other words, we develop the plan today based on the information we have available today. Tomorrow, as we get additional information, we update the plan. Planning is an ongoing process.

Execute

Then we have to take action. This is a test of our faith. Take a step forward and work the plan. As we execute the plan, we learn more from the experience and continue updating the plan and working the plan until we reach our goal, destination, or objective.

In addition, we must work and develop a positive attitude and optimism. Attitude and optimism are the emotional glue that help us bring it and keep it all together: the belief, the plan, and the execution.

As we plan and work with optimism and enthusiasm, we will get better at developing the required skills, and as a result, we will become better and better. This activity and practice will help us develop confidence. Confidence and competence will come as the result of these elements. The results of all these efforts will be the achievement of our goals.

My oldest daughter, Rosemarie, gave me a beautiful frame for Father's Day some years back. It contains a famous quote attributed to President Theodore Roosevelt: "Believe you can—and you're halfway there." I love the message, and I know it is true because I have personally experienced it in my life.

The first part of the message is the "believe" part. This part includes the dreaming, the imagining, the researching, the seeking counsel, and all the other elements that are part of using our minds to give shape to what we want to accomplish in life. This part includes the planning, which is the outlining and documenting of the steps necessary for the transformation of the dreams, goals, and aspirations into real and concrete realities in our lives.

The second half is the doing. In business, it is often referred to as the execution of the plan. The transformation of our plan into action will lead to victory, conquest, and achievement of that what we seek to realize or obtain.

It is critically important to make every effort to do what we say we are going to do. We have to do what we say we are going to do. If we want our confidence to grow, we must make every effort to do as we say we are going to do. The best way to achieve what we what we seek is to follow a written plan for what we want to accomplish. This will help us in many ways. It will help us make corrections and improve our approaches. It will help us learn about what works and what does not work in the circumstances we face every day. It will also help us when we fail. We must make corrections to our plans or make brand-new plans if necessary.

Execution is about *doing*. Execution is about following a plan that we have developed. Execution is about following the script we prepared for achievement.

I am a big fan of the Star Wars universe and all its stories, characters, and lessons. I found important messages in the stories of the characters. One of the messages was given to Luke Skywalker by Master Yoda while Luke was being trained as a Jedi in the swamp on the Dagobah planet, which was home to Yoda in his final years. The message from Yoda to Luke was quite simple: There is no middle ground. "Either we do or we do not." This is worth repeating over and over. There is no middle ground. There is no try. Either we do or we do not do. Therefore, execution is about staying with the goal and plan until we reach the goal.

One of my mentors—individuals who influence us in positive

- Finding My Purpose, Finding My Way in Life -

ways and help us define who we are and where we are going—was a rear admiral I had the blessing of working for in a support capacity. He impressed me from the moment I had the honor and pleasure of meeting him. He came into our organization and immediately shared with us his first ninety-day plan. He was prepared to lead our organization even before he started. He had studied our organization's needs and prepared an important ninety-day plan that defined how we would move forward during his tenure. Before the end of his first ninety days, he had prepared a five-year strategy, a twelve-month plan, and another ninety-day plan and goals. This had a very positive effect in our organization. It gave us a clear view of our path forward. The plans were very important, but, equally important were the ways we moved to execute the plans we had set out to do.

The admiral shared stories with us about experiences during his career. One of the stories that had a great impact in my life was the story of a sign: "It can be done." As a young officer, he had worked in the White House for the president of the United States. The sign posted on the president's desk—"It can be done"—reflected that the holder of the office was a firm believer of the fact that everything is possible.

Although he believed that everything was possible, he required that any matter that was brought to him had the following elements: researching the challenge—getting all the facts and bringing the evidence—and identifying all the alternatives. He also required that the best alternatives be presented to him with confidence. He challenged everyone to be prepared to act, determine the best way to solve the problem, and bring about the improvements for whatever the circumstances called for. He placed emphasis on both the preparation and the execution and lived by the theme "It can be done" all his life.

When I was a small child, I used to think that life was so big and overwhelming. However, as I have grown and learned through my own experiences and the experiences of others, I have come to realize that it is true: It can be done. Everything is possible. All things can be done.

> But Jesus looked at them and said to them, "With men this is impossible, but with God all things are possible." (Matthew 19:26)

We must seek Him and place our lives and all our affairs on His hands, and He will give us whatever is required to accomplish whatever we set out to do in our lives.

It is a matter of breaking down the big goals into small pieces and working on each small piece one at a time. If I want to lose twelve pounds in the next three months, that means four pounds each month or one pound per week. If I am taking a class, and it takes six weeks to complete six units, one per week, then tackle one unit per week and then break down each unit into seven small parts, one for each day. To do one small part of the unit a day—completing one unit per week—you need to plan each week on a weekly calendar. This example can help develop good study habits.

These are some techniques, tips, and habits that must be developed over time to be the best student you can be, in the classroom, online, or in life in general:

- When taking a class or pursuing a degree or certification in a particular field, study the overall program before you start:

  - How many classes do I need?
  - When are they offered?
  - How much is it going to cost?
  - How am I going to pay for it?

- Determine the planned start date and planned end date.
- Sit in the front of the classroom or conference room:
  - Pay attention
  - Take notes
  - Participate in discussions
- Read the notes you take in class.
- Start assignments early.
- Break down assignments and projects into small parts.
- Make a plan of how to complete the assignments and projects.
- What can I realistically complete every day to complete this plan?
- What research is required?
- Communicate with your professor or instructor and seek help when in doubt.
- Share information with classmates when possible—we can learn from each other.
- Collaborate with others and seek help.
- Stay seated during the project, study, and make whatever effort is required until you finish. Stay focused until you complete the task, assignment, or project.

Tools can help us with the execution and realization of our plans, goals, and aspirations. A carpenter needs good tools to construct and create things, and as we become good planners, we will discover good planning tools that can help us document our plans, track our progress, and realize what we seek to accomplish.

Planning Tools

Write things down. I always have my daily planner and plain paper and a pencil to take notes, capture my thoughts, and schedule what I would like to get done ahead of time.

Photos

Take photographs of the things you desire: a car, a house, a family, a wedding, a trip, a college degree. See yourself already in possession of what you desire—in harmony with the Lord's will.

These tools are available for planning our time and projects, and they keep us on track to execute our plans and achieve our objectives. Simple planning tools can help us write down our plans, organize our thoughts and ideas, and break them down into actionable tasks so we can track our progress and measure our progress toward the achievement of our goals.

Outlook Calendar

Outlook Calendar has a great management function. It is just one example we may use. It can be used in conjunction with a daily planner. We can use an electronic daily planner or an electronic calendar to keep track of our appointments and tasks we want to accomplish as we work toward realizing our goals. There are many versions of electronic calendars and paper calendars and planners. This is a personal choice. The important thing is to develop the habit of planning ahead, one day at a time, one week at a time, one month a time, one year at a time, and so on.

Outlook Task-Management Function

We can also use Outlook to keep track of tasks we can manage daily, weekly, monthly, or yearly. We need to use the planner, calendar, or task-management application on a daily basis and keep it up to date. We must develop the habit to dedicate the first efforts of our day to reviewing our plans for the day, week, or month to be certain about where we are today and what we want to accomplish to get us closer to the achievement of our goals.

Six-Week Class Planning Calendar

This is another example of a simple planning tool. For example, we can use the MS Excel application and develop a calendar on a spreadsheet. This could be for a six-week class. This calendar can be easily constructed with information extracted from the class syllabus, which should contain the class agenda for each week. With this information, we can build a day-by-day plan. The goal is to follow this weekly plan, day by day, to make sure we complete all the class assignments and requirements, thereby obtaining good results.

Microsoft Excel and a Weekly Calendar

We can use this powerful application to develop a calendar to track established weekly milestones. It can allow us to look at the entire week and schedule when deliverables need to be completed. It can be used as a guide to help us stay on track, one week at a time, until we successfully finish the project's objectives.

Simple Project Management and Planning Tools

MS Excel can also be used to make a task list and track our progress every day. It is an excellent tool for keeping track of projects. It is a great tool that we can use for small or large projects. There are many project management software applications that are more sophisticated, but I find a simple spreadsheet is easy to keep up to date as we move forward and work the plan. We can use Excel with Microsoft Office's applications such as Word or PowerPoint. Apple's Numbers application is a very good tool. On the Mac, we can use the spreadsheet application Numbers in conjunction with Letters and Keynote for documents and presentations.

Planning and Personal Management Systems

Paper-based planners can be also very effective. These are tools we can use to develop the habit to plan every day—even on our days off. There are many examples of calendars we can use. Some of the most popular planning systems are Day Timer or Franklin Covey. They are very similar, but Franklin Covey has many more time management accessories and inspirational messages.

Planning Binders

Some individuals and organizations use planning binders. The idea is to organize all the information, including images, photos, statistics, studies, and proposals together with all the stated requirements of our goals. We can use a binder to organize the plan, reference materials, and other documents necessary to accomplish the goals outlined inside. It is a working tool. This means that we need to review this binder regularly and make updates as necessary until the goals are achieved. Again, it is critical that we develop the habit to set up a binder for each project. Because the binder is a planning tool, we must continuously review the binder and update the binder with new information as we receive it. This is a great tool to prepare our plan, monitor our progress for each project, and work the plan until we achieve our goals and objectives. The binders will help us stay organized, focused, and on target.

Palm trees and blue skies by the bay

When He had stopped speaking, He said to Simon, "Launch out into the deep and let down your nets for a catch." But Simon answered and said to Him, "Master, we have toiled all night and caught nothing; nevertheless at Your word I will let down the net." And when they had done this, they caught a great number of fish, and their net was breaking.
—Luke 5:4–7

CHAPTER 6

Staying Focused

Trust the Lord. Trust the Word of the Lord. Peter learned to trust the Lord and followed His guidance in life. We need to learn to develop our faith and trust the Lord in all things in life. In order to stay focused in life, we must learn to trust the Lord, trust His gifts to us, and trust our abilities to accomplish the things we have set out to do.

Peter walked on water—on top of the water that is—because he was focused on the Lord.

The Bible is full of great stories of great individuals who submitted their lives to the Lord and were able to accomplish the impossible. The Bible is full of great promises from the Lord about His love and direction to us. He promises to guide us and to be with us always:

> The secret of the Lord is with those who fear Him, And He will show them His covenant. My eyes are ever toward the Lord, For He shall pluck my feet out of the net. (Psalm 25:14–15)

By keeping our eyes on the Lord, He will deliver us from whatever challenges or difficulties we may face. It is really that simple.

This same principle was portrayed in Peter's experience when the disciples were on a boat during a storm. They were afraid they were going to drown, but Jesus came walking on water toward them. At first, they were afraid and thought He was a ghost.

Peter knew Jesus is Lord and asked the Lord to allow him to come toward him:

> But immediately Jesus spoke to them, saying, "Be of good cheer! It is I; do not be afraid."
>
> And Peter answered Him and said, "Lord, if it is You, command me to come to You on the water."
>
> So He said, "Come." And when Peter had come down out of the boat, he walked on the water to go to Jesus. But when he saw that the wind was boisterous, he was afraid; and beginning to sink he cried out, saying, "Lord, save me!" (Matthew 14:27–30)

Jesus said to Peter, "Come."

Peter was heavier than water, and it was not physically possible for him to walk on water. This verse does not say that Peter floated; it says that Peter walked on water. The power of Jesus Christ made it possible for Peter to walk on water.

While he stayed focused on the Lord, he walked on water. Peter did something that is humanly impossible. With God's help, as Peter did, we can also do impossible things.

The moment Peter lost focus, when he took his eyes from the Lord and looked at his circumstances instead of staying focused on the Lord, he started to sink. Only when Jesus extended His hand to Peter was he able to stop sinking, and he was saved from drowning.

Peter failed the moment he took his eyes off the Lord.

Failure in life is constant because we are imperfect creatures. However, if we choose to do so, we can learn through failure and persevere and strengthen our resolve. Therefore, failure is an important part of our learning process. However, we need to work hard to minimize the failures as we mature. Ideally, our long-term goal should be to eliminate failures altogether. Nevertheless, we have to accept the fact that we are not perfect and are constantly battling our own weaknesses. Only God is perfect, but in the manner in which we draw our lives closer to Him, we will do extraordinary things, through the power of the Holy Spirit and for the glory of the Lord.

In terms of failure, what is more important to grasp is the need to immediately recognize failure and get to work promptly on a recovery effort that will glorify our Father by the things we do, achieving victory in the face of defeat.

Merriam-Webster defines focus as "a state or condition permitting clear perception or understanding" or "direction."

This can only be achieved by regularly reviewing our goals, strategies, and plans. Regularly reviewing, studying, and meditating on our goals allows us to develop a clear picture of who we are and where we are going. The element of praying about our goals and plans is a critical part of this process. Through prayer, we place all our goals, dreams, aspirations, and strategies in the Lord's hands. Only God knows exactly what is going to happen tomorrow. Nevertheless, through prayer, we come humbly before the Father and ask for the wisdom and courage to do His will in whatever we dedicate our lives to doing. This process requires ongoing and constant communication and communion with the Father. We must do this every day.

Paul says, "Pray without ceasing" (1 Thessalonians 5:17). This means praying constantly.

Prayer is not limited by time or space. Therefore, we need not to be at a church or place of worship to pray. In fact, we must make an effort to constantly pray; it does not matter where we are. We can pray when we get up in the morning or while we ride the train or bus or drive to work or school. We can have a few moments of prayer when we arrive to the office or classroom. We can pray while we exercise, run, or walk. We can pray in front of a lake or an ocean. We can pray when we fly in an airplane. We can pray when we ride our bicycles. The Lord is everywhere. He listens to us, and He listens to our hearts and minds. He knows all things. However, He wants us to come to Him via prayer, humbly, and place our souls in His hands constantly—like Hannah did.

In the book of 1 Samuel, we learn about a woman who knew the Lord, and she was aware of her purpose in life. She wanted to be a mother.

Being a mother was fundamentally important in her culture, but she was sterile. She was not able to produce children. She was focused on being a mother and did not stop until she accomplished her purpose in life—for the Lord's glory.

Even though her soul was full of sorrow because she could not conceive, she knew that all things are possible for God. Hannah went to the Lord in prayer and placed her desire in the Lord's hands. The Word says that Hannah "poured" her soul before the Lord:

> And Hannah answered and said, "No, my lord, I am a woman of a sorrowful spirit: I have drunk neither wine nor strong drink, but have poured out my soul before the Lord." (1 Samuel 1:15)

The Lord listened to Hannah's prayer. He intervened in Hannah's life in a miraculous way because the Lord had a great purpose for Hannah's life and the child who was to come from her. Hannah promised to dedicate this child to the Lord.

In the same manner, the Lord will also listen to our prayers and intervene in our lives in miraculous ways. Trust the Lord. His Love endures forever. He has joy in giving to His sons and daughters what we ask, when we pour our souls in the Lord's hands just like Hannah did. Let's dedicate our lives and purpose in service to the Lord.

Hannah had a conversation with a priest:

And she said, "Oh my lord, as thy soul liveth, my lord, I am the woman that stood by thee here, praying unto the Lord. For this child I prayed; and the Lord hath given me my petition which I asked of him." (1 Samuel 1:26–27)

The Lord answered Hannah's prayer in a powerful way, and a great prophet was born by the grace of God.

Many things are written about what prayer is. There are also many good books about prayer. Praying is, among many things, about worshipping the Lord, asking for forgiveness, placing our desires in the Lord's hands, and asking and receiving.

One of the most critical petitions we must constantly have before the Lord is asking for wisdom and strength. Wisdom is the knowledge of what to do or say and having the strength and courage to stay focused on whatever endeavor we are involved in. We can only achieve this condition of clear perception and understanding with the presence of the Holy Spirit in our lives.

According to Dr. Norman Vincent Peale, the Lord has a great sense of humor. When he has great blessings for us, it usually means we also are going to have great problems and great challenges. However, problems and difficulties are an integral part of the blessing because problems and difficulties strengthen resolve and build character so we can learn to be perseverant, rise above the trials, and show others the awesome power of our Father and Lord, Jesus Christ!

When we are able to focus on a goal, we then are able to develop *persistence*. *Merriam-Webster* defines persistence as the action or act of persisting. Persistence is related to perseverance, which is the continued effort to do or achieve something despite difficulties, failure, or opposition.

We need to stay focused on our goals and purpose in life. We need to be persistent, develop perseverance, overcome, and achieve what we are here to do.

Here are some examples of ordinary individuals, characters, and creatures—created in God's image—I have learned about and come to admire:

President Abraham Lincoln

He focused his life on keeping our great nation united. He asked and obtained the help of thousands who spilled their blood and gave their lives for the object of their focus.

General Douglas MacArthur

He was focused, like our entire nation was, on defeating the Japanese army, defending the Pacific, and bringing peace to the world.

Dwight D. Eisenhower

He was focused on winning the war and defeating the mighty armies of the Third Reich. He was focused on uniting the Allies into one extraordinary force that could accomplish the impossible.

Roberto Clemente

He was focused on being the best right fielder for the Pittsburgh Pirates. This Hall of Fame baseball player had three thousand career hits. While doing all this, this handsome kid from the Borinquen was focused in caring for his fellow humans and helping those around him in times of need. He died while focusing on accomplishing his purpose.

Michael Jordan

He was focused on flying while playing basketball for the Chicago Bulls. He was focused on winning NBA championships and inspiring others to do the same.

Steve Jobs

He was focused on making computers an appliance and creating devices of great beauty, quality, and utility. He was focused on making devices that required people to "Think Different" and doing the impossible by placing a thousand songs in our pockets.

Gandhi

He was focused on bringing political change to a great nation in a peaceful manner. In the process, he also impacted all of us with his belief in the possibility of peace, love, and understanding while standing tall for human rights and dignity.

Mother Teresa

She was focused on serving the poor and hungry under the most challenging of circumstances. Her focus is a great example of tenacity and the beauty of doing God's will in everyday life.

President John F. Kennedy

Among other things, he challenged Americans to go to the moon. Our nation was focused on accomplishing the dream of reaching the moon in ten years. He challenged us with this extraordinary thought of doing the impossible. Americans focused on the goal, on the dream, and in 1968, the dream became real.

I could go on and on with other examples of individuals who were able to focus on extraordinary goals and achieve them. They left extraordinary marks on life and impacted others in many positive ways.

How will my life impact others in a good way? How can I focus my energy to realize my goals and do good for others? By serving. We serve others and serve the Lord every day with what we think, what we speak, and what we do.

Fall colors by the lake

To everything there is a season, and a time
to every purpose under the heaven.
—Ecclesiastes 3:1

CHAPTER 7

The Stages of Life

Why am I here? Look at creation. Everything around us has a purpose. The trees, the birds, the reptiles, the fish, and all matter around us have a purpose. Look and study the chemicals that make up creation from living to inert matter. All these chemicals exist to fulfill a purpose. There is plenty of scientific evidence that supports this statement.

There are many things in the universe we still know nothing about, but the more we discover, the more we are able to understand how things are made and connected. The more I read and learn about science, the more I am able to understand and clearly see this reality around everything I do and everything I am. I am able to see God's hand and God's love all around the universe.

We are here to grow, learn, and produce fruit. That is why we are here. In producing fruit, we spread God's power and love all around us. We are seeds, and we come from seeds. We are seeds with the potential to grow into big trees and to be a source of good in the universe. Seeds are meant to grow and produce fruit. We can produce shade even if we do not produce fruit for the birds and other animals to eat. We are here to provide wood for housing. We are here to provide wood to burn to cook our food and produce warmth when it is cold. There are many similarities between humans and other elements of creation. The universe is all around us.

- Finding My Purpose, Finding My Way in Life -

How do we produce fruit? By serving others. When we give a smile, a hug, or a helping hand of any kind. By listening to others when they are in pain. By teaching others, we produce fruit. By giving our time, money, and other resources so others may benefit in some way. We are fed back and receive as a result of what we give, what we provide, and what we share.

We are born from the seeds of two individuals. It is a miracle, a never-ending marvelous process how an individual develops from two seeds with traits from their mother, their father, and their ancestors. The new creature is physiologically, emotionally, and spiritually unique. It is a miracle that many do not quite understand. This is the stage of life from which we start developing and growing.

We go through stages of growth from the start. The seeds grow into a fetus, and then we arrive in the world as newborns. We develop into curious creatures during the "terrible twos." After the toddler stage comes the young child stage. We continue to absorb from our environments and develop. Then we become older children and a preteens. We go through a very turbulent growth stage as teenagers. In this stage, boys and girls change dramatically—physically and emotionally. This stage of growth can be difficult, and some do not make it because of confusion and lack of good models to follow, among many other factors that influence our growth. After the challenging growth stage of adolescence, we become young adults.

Each step of growth brings new challenges that are designed to help us continue on our path through life until we complete our mission on this planet. During each stage, we learn when we choose to do so. This learning requires us to become humble and submit to a higher purpose. This certainly helps us move toward self-actualization, which is the realization of our full potential. It is becoming the best we can be.

We go through growing stages. We are designed to go through this painful process by expanding, reaching, learning, and extending ourselves to the next level. Growth is always challenging, but it is full of opportunities for learning, strengthening character, and helping us define who we are and why we are here.

We learn through all our senses in every experience in life. We are in a constant state of learning: young mature adult, mature adult, senior citizen, and then elder. Maturity means having completed natural growth and development or having attained a final or desired state of full development.

Seek growth at every stage. Learn, contribute, share, and help others at every stage.

To grow is to have the opportunity to take on new challenges and responsibilities.

In *This is How We Grow*, Dr. Christina Hibbert teaches about growing, overcoming, becoming, and flourishing:

> To me, personal growth includes all of these things. It means choosing to remain open and receive the lessons we are given: choosing to learn from whatever comes our way. I've been handed many life experiences that have given me opportunities to grow, several of which I write about in my memoir, *This is How We Grow*. As I write, "There is a reason for every season of growth ... 'Life is Change. Growth is optional. Choose wisely.'[1] What will your choice be? I choose to grow" (5).

To me, this says it all. We are each given opportunities to learn and grow—some we want, and some we do not want—but it's up to us to decide what to do with it.

Thus, *personal growth* is a process of identifying the physical, emotional, mental, social, and spiritual changes we desire and working in each area to improve and reach our fullest potential. And this, essentially, is self-actualization.

Merriam-Webster defines self-actualization as "fully realizing one's potential." I cannot tell you what your full potential is or what

- Finding My Purpose, Finding My Way in Life -

it can be. This is something you must find on your own through the development of a personal relationship with our Lord and Savior Jesus Christ. This will come through the development of a life of prayer, meditation, and the study of the Word of God. It will be revealed to us in no uncertain terms. God speaks to us in many ways. He will always listen to our prayers, and He will always answer our prayers.

Jesus told us about the power of believing:

> Jesus said unto him, If thou canst believe, all things are possible to him that believeth. (Mark 9:23)

God calls us to believe big, think big, pray big, plan big, and act big. The Lord is a big Lord. He is the *greatest* authority in the universe. Through His Word, all things were created. His Love is big and infinite. His love is big, infinite, and forever. The Lord's love is so big that He gave His only Son to die for us on the cross, so whosoever believes in Him, you and I, and everyone who believes in Him, shall not perish but have everlasting life. Glory be to God:

> For God so loved the world, that he gave his only begotten Son, that whosoever believeth in him should not perish, but have everlasting life. (John 3:16)

And then go on into eternity. In terms of the soul, it is the quality or state of being eternal. Our ultimate destiny is to be with the Lord through eternity if we believe in Him and surrender our lives and our purpose to Him—or have eternal death separated from the Lord.

While we are here in this planet, we are called to grow, contribute, and provide fruit, which will impact others all throughout our existence. What we do impacts others in many ways.

The following is a famous line from the opening scene Ridley

Scott's award-winning *Gladiator*. They are in northern Europe, far from the Roman Empire's capital in the warm climate of Rome. It is winter and very cold in Germany. The mighty Roman army is in front of the last stand of the German opposition. The Germans did not know they were already conquered, which General Maximus points out to one of his generals. The Romans sent an emissary to the Germans, but they sent him back decapitated. This marked the time to begin the last battle.

General Maximus tells his men that what is about to happen is of great significance. He tells them that we must give the best of who we are to whatever it is we do. General Maximus tells his troops to remember that they may die in battle but to give their best. "Whatever we do in life, echoes into eternity." We are here today, and then we are gone. We do not know when or how our time on this planet will come to an end. Therefore, we most rejoice every day and do the best we can. Whatever we do, we must make every effort to give it our best. Everything we do, we must do to the max because, ultimately, we are doing it for our Lord.

King Solomon was a seeker of wisdom. He asked God for wisdom, and the Lord gave him wisdom. King Solomon was confronted with the task of managing the people of the kingdom of Israel, and he knew it was a very difficult task. He was young and did not know how to lead his people. Therefore, he humbled himself before the Lord and asked Him for the wisdom to be a good leader and manage the people of Israel.

He asked the Lord for wisdom to be a good steward with God's purpose for his life, and the Lord gave him wisdom and many other resources to fulfill his purpose:

> I know that nothing is better for them than to rejoice
> and to do good in their lives. (Ecclesiastes 3:12)

Therefore, we must seek the Lord in all we do. This is the beginning of wisdom. We must be brave and face all our circumstances

- Finding My Purpose, Finding My Way in Life -

with the confidence that the Lord is with us, and we will always find alternatives to the challenges we face. And then we must do this with joy, knowing that in each challenge we face, we have the choice to grow or not. We must choose to grow because this is God's will for our lives. In doing the Lord's will, we will find joy and fulfillment.

Fall is not the end; it is the beginning. It is the start of new things. In order to have spring and summer, we must first go through fall and winter.

I was born in a tropical island paradise. Although I visited New York City when I was a teenager on various occasions, it was always during summer. Therefore, I experienced the hot summer weather with plenty of sunshine. I saw light and the spectacle of blue skies and green vegetation in the various parks of the city and upstate New York.

When I was drafted in the US Army in September 1972, I came face-to-face with fall. Earth is tilting, and the Northern Hemisphere is farther from the sun; therefore, it gets cold. It was gray and cold, and I could see all the dark clouds over me. I could feel the cold and the absence of sunshine in my life.

For various reasons, I had failed in college. After three years at the University of Puerto Rico's College of Engineers and Surveyors, I had a terrible grade point average. I was told I could not continue to be student there. Many factors led to those disastrous results, but I took responsibility because it was my life. Ultimately, it was my job to face my circumstances and overcome them. I did not overcome the obstacles I faced in college. I made destructive choices that led to my failure. It was a very depressing time for me, and I was trying to blame every individual on this planet—except me—for this defeat. I was not able to talk about this episode of my life for some time.

Then something extraordinary happened. The Vietnam conflict had been going on for more than eight years. The United States was involved because the French had their Vietnam conflict before.

Our military intervention in Southeast Asia was not very popular. The people of the United States were mostly against the military conflict. Georgie Jimenez, a friend since first grade, was drafted as soon as he got out of high school. He came back in a casket draped with the American flag.

My cousin Angel got drafted and became a medic in an infantry unit. He served one tour, and when the time came, he reenlisted. He went back to Vietnam to help our brothers and sisters who were dying there. He shared some of his experiences there. When he started to talk about them, he could not stop crying—and I would cry with him.

Only by the grace of God I was spared from going to Vietnam. When I was called to serve as a result of a selective service lottery system that was implemented to make our military services a volunteer service force.

On September 26, 1972, at 4:00 a.m., my father drove me to Fort Brooks in San Juan, and I was inducted into the United States Army. It was a dark time in my life. I was not aware of the honor that was vested in me to be part of this legendary organization. I felt like dark times were upon me when I arrived for basic training in Fort Jackson, South Carolina. They cut my hair and dressed me the same as everybody else. I felt I had been robbed of my personality, which added to me depression. It was fall, it was gray, and it was cold. I wrote letters to my mother, my grandmother, my father, my sisters, and even my dog. I was too ashamed to write to my former girlfriend, but I wanted badly to write to her. That was a grave mistake for which I would lose sleep for the rest of my life.

My first physical exercises were very painful. I was totally out of shape, and I could not run with a thirty-five-pound bag on my back and combat boots. I was punished by my drill sergeant for getting out of formation while running because I was completely out of breath. I was told that the drill sergeants were going to transform me and make me a soldier whether I cooperated or not.

After various grueling punishments where I ate sand and dirt, I decided that I wanted to get on with the program and be a soldier. I prayed, and God gave me strength. When my basic training

- Finding My Purpose, Finding My Way in Life -

concluded, on graduation day, twelve weeks later, I was sharply dressed on my dress green uniform and ran several miles when the ceremony ended. It was December 1972, and I was a sharp soldier in the United States Army.

From there, I was sent to the US Army Communications School in Fort Monmouth, New Jersey. Because of my academic experience, I was sent to advanced individual training as a field communications specialist. That was my introduction to electronics, transistors, and elementary computing. When my training was complete, I was assigned to the Signal Company, Support Battalion, Seventh Special Forces Group, at Fort Bragg, North Carolina. This was an honor vested on me and an assignment of great responsibility.

During the dark days in the fall of 1972, the seeds of a great experience were planted in my life. I went on to complete my active-duty service and the US Army Reserve, and I received an honorable discharge in September 1978. My faithful and honorable service was rewarded by a grateful nation in many ways.

These are some of the benefits I received as a result of my efforts and service as a United States Army soldier. I became fit, and I developed a lifelong consciousness of being fit. The exercise helped me be the best I could ever be physically by running five miles comfortably, doing sit-ups, push-ups, monkey bars, and other exercises.

I was able to get a good job in Chicago with a great and prestigious organization because of my military service during the Vietnam era. This event influenced my character and shaped my business management career forever.

I was able to go back to college and earn a bachelor's degree with good grades because my GI Bill benefits paid the way.

My military experience influenced my character in a way that helped me live my life with better choices. I will always be a soldier.

Looking back on my life, I see the different seasons clearly marked with winter storms, summer storms, tropical storms, days of sunshine, colorful spring days, days of summer heat, and seeds planted in me by my Lord. Sometimes I produced good fruit, and sometimes I did not.

Each experience in our lives is a seed to use and become the best we can be. The more I am willing to do to be the best I can be, to grow and produce great things, the more I am able to help others and impact the world around me.

This is an important part of God's will in our lives. Let's look at the different seasons in life as opportunities to help the seeds of greatness grow in us and around us in all the people the Lord places in our path.

The planting of vines

But others fell on good ground and yielded a crop:
some a hundredfold, some sixty, some thirty.
He who has ears to hear, let him hear!
—Matthew 13:8–9

CHAPTER 8

Remain Teachable

According to *Merriam-Webster*, the simple definition of the word *teachable* is "able and willing to learn: capable of being taught."

> Whoso loveth instruction loveth knowledge: but he that hateth reproof is brutish. (Proverbs 12:1)

When we are open-minded and humble to receive new instructions about many things, we will receive knowledge and wisdom. Having an open mind and the will to learn will take us to new levels of understanding. This is a critical element to our continuous process of growing as individuals. It requires that we humble ourselves to the fact that we are acquiring new information and new knowledge.

When we do not like to receive instructions because we believe we already know everything, we become foolish and ignorant.

I went to a customer services excellence class sponsored by my employer. When I was told I had to go to the class, I thought, *What do I need another customer service class for? I know everything about customer services there is to know. I have taken many customer services classes throughout my career. I have had thousands of great customer services experiences during my career. I trained hundreds of employees the art and tactics of good service. In fact, I learned my first lessons* on customer services as a small child when I observed my grandfather working on his general store and taking care of his customers in a very polite way. He was very kind and very respectful of others. It had a profound influence in my life. I know everything about customer services.

I was in for a great surprise. I was wrong—there is so much more I can learn about service excellence.

Learning is a continuous and never-ending process. In the same manner as the concept of growth all around us in all living things, learning is part of who we are and how we grow.

The instructor was a very impressive individual. We were introduced to his academic and professional accomplishments in a humble way. He had a powerful control of the subject of service excellence. His confidence was built upon the fact that he knows the subject very well. His confidence made a powerful statement as he delivered the content, and we absorbed the material.

Everything he was doing was part of the service he was providing to us—the students—by delivering the message in a way that we were impacted positively. We all retained the lessons we learned. Service is all about the things we do in helping others. Whether we are public servants, health professionals, or engaged in another endeavor, we are required to serve others.

During his class, we visited many of the customer services concepts I had learned through a lifetime of serving in different contexts. The class was a refresher and an opportunity to learn and understand how servicing others makes us grow and improve. We receive many good things physically, emotionally, and spiritually.

Charles Ward said, "The common finding is the people who invest in others experience better health, live longer, and enjoy their lives more than people who do not" (15). Various studies show that individuals who choose to serve others with joy and peace in their hearts tend to live fuller lives and have more rewarding careers.

This is a great example, and we have many others that clearly demonstrate the fact that we must remain humble throughout life. We must have a clear understanding of the fact that we do not know everything there is to know. Only God has all the knowledge. We must continue to learn and grow every day until our journeys on this planet come to an end:

> And be not conformed to this world: but be ye transformed by the renewing of your mind, that ye may prove what is that good, and acceptable, and perfect, will of God. (Romans 12:2)

We have a responsibility to stay alert and constantly seek ways to gain access to new information, new ideas, and new ways of looking at different subjects. This contributes to the renewal of our minds with what is good, acceptable, and perfect.

There are many things we can do in order to accomplish this. One of my preferred ways is constantly studying the Holy Book. The Bible is God's Word, and it is timeless. In other words, it is always fresh in its messages to us. Together with a life of prayer and meditation, the study of the Bible will move us to higher levels of understanding and help us grow in our spiritual lives. It will also help us grow emotionally and physically.

As we mature, we can continue to learn and grow in many ways. We can attend conferences on topics that interest us, take college courses, read books, and have conversations with others who can contribute to our growth. We can also contribute to their growth. The idea is to remain open-minded and teachable. We do not know everything there is to know. We must remain teachable. We must understand that there are multiple perspectives and different points of view for all subjects in life. When we stand where others stand and look at the subjects from other people's points of view, we may see the subject in a slightly different light.

This is part of God's will. He wants to see us grow as we progress in life. At some point, we will produce fruit that others may benefit from as well.

A recent reality TV show featured a group of volunteers who

would spend sixty days in prison as observers. Apparently, these images were planted in my mind in such a way that I had a dream that night about going to jail. It was a great example of the way our environment, what we see, who we share our lives with, and all the things we are exposed to can influence us.

In my dream, I entered the jail with a Bible under my arm. I immediately was faced with very strong and tall individuals with tattoos all over their bodies. I said, "I greet you with joy because my Lord has a purpose for bringing me here. He wants me to share the love, the power, the hope, the freedom, and the truth which is written in this book." I shared some passages from the Holy Book, the Word of God. The Holy Spirit was with me.

From then on, I walked through the jail with the confidence to teach others about the Holy Book. I told those who wanted to hear that all of us are sinners. We all have flaws brought about by sin, but God loved us in such a way that He gave his only Son. If we believe in Him, we shall be forgiven and have eternal life.

With the strength and wisdom of the Holy Spirit, I was able to show others God's love, mercy, and forgiveness—no matter our circumstances. When we seek the Lord, we will find Him and He will receive us with open arms.

I engaged those who really wanted to come to the Lord and started various programs to teach inmates to read. We developed another program to teach music and found instruments. The Lord provided. We also developed a music group. We developed music courses and taught some of them how to play musical instruments. We made musical arrangements, engaged in rehearsals, and delivered an extraordinary message of hope through music.

We also developed a Bible study group. We studied together, prayed, shared experiences, and learned to meditate on God's Word and His promises. We also learned to fast. We taught and learned and experienced the presence of the Holy Spirit in our lives. Lives were transformed.

When I woke up, I understood that I needed to always remain

teachable. Even if I went to jail for some mistake I made, I could be an instrument of God's love, mercy, forgiveness, awesome power, wisdom, and provision. Even in the worst of circumstances, we will find blessings if we surrender our lives to God.

Therefore, we must make an effort to remain teachable and grow. It does not matter where we are because the Lord has a purpose for everything in the universe, which is His creation.

It was just a dream, but I believe the Lord used this experience to teach me and expand my comprehension of His love. He loves me, and all He wants me to do is to surrender to Him and do His will. When we do this, our will merges with God's will—and then extraordinary things happen in our lives and all around us. When we do this, the impossible becomes possible, walls are taken down, and miracles come to pass all around us.

Remaining teachable includes being humble. Merriam Webster defines humble as "reflecting, expressing, or offered in a spirit of deference or submission." To me, the best example of "humble" was Jesus since He submitted himself to doing God's will and going through the passion of the Christ.

Jesus's triumphantly and defiantly entered Jerusalem. He knew He was going to face His enemies and find certain death on the cross. He was not riding a white horse with an army of warriors or angels; he was riding a small donkey. The Son of God, King of kings, Lord of lords chose to ride a donkey. This was a demonstration of humbleness and submission to the utmost authority. The Father sustains the stars out of nothingness. Jesus submitted His will to the Father's will out of love, which is the most powerful force in the universe.

Because of His humbleness and submission to the Lord's will, Jesus was raised from the dead and glorified. He now sits at the right side of the Father. Humbleness and submission will bring blessings from the Lord that are beyond our comprehension.

The ultimate humbleness is submission to our Lord and Savior and Father. He is the ultimate and greatest authority in the universe.

- Finding My Purpose, Finding My Way in Life -

To be humble does not mean having low self-esteem and allowing others and circumstances to destroy us or treat us disrespectfully.

I have witnessed many individuals mistaking humbleness for something else.

Humbleness is related with the concept of awareness. To be humble we have to be aware. Deepak Chopra MD, FACP, one of the greatest thinkers of our time, wrote about why consciousness is the biggest secret to success."(17)

> In order to understand awareness seriously, we must ask ourselves these questions: Who am I?, What do I want?, and What does this situation demand? This requires a constant analysis of where we are at a particular moment and time in our lives. It is also referred to as situational awareness. Sometimes it is also referred to as perspective of our current position in life. Understanding who we are means getting to know where we come from and where we are going. It also requires that we have an understanding of our strengths and weaknesses. In order to be able to transform ourselves from where we are to where we want to be we must know where we are right now. This requires humbleness.

Humbleness is about understanding that we are a small part of this infinite universe while understanding that we were created in God's image—and the Spirit of the Lord is with us. Both things are true.

The opposite of humbleness is arrogance. It says, "I am above my circumstances, and I will overcome because of my own strengths. I do not need anything or anybody because I am self-sufficient." This type of thinking may get results in the short term, but it will surely bring failure and emptiness in the long term.

The Creator gave all of us curiosity to make sure we grow all the way to the end of our existence on this planet. Some of us are more curious than others. The more challenging our purpose, the more curious we are required to be. As we grow and go through the different stages in life, curiosity will play a critical part in moving us toward gaining knowledge, maturity, and wisdom.

Our most important relationship in life is our relationship with our Father and Lord Jesus Christ. When we truly understand the importance of our relationship with God, we will be more curious about His love, power, mercy, forgiveness, and His most precious gift to us: life everlasting in His presence.

The more we are able to comprehend God's love and power, the more we will be able to share with others during our lives:

> Neither pray I for these alone, but for them also which shall believe on me through their word. (John 17:20)

Jesus is looking into the future and telling us in His prayer to the Father about all the ones who would come because the disciples would spread Jesus's message of love, power, and hope around the known world of the time. This is also talking about those who believe in Him, are actively spreading the Lord's message, and will help others come to know the Lord.

It is imperative that we seek the presence of the Lord in our lives through the study of His Word, prayer, meditation, and through making a sincere effort every day to live our lives honoring Him and being a good example to others. This does not mean we will live perfect lives. We are at war with a spiritual world focused of robing our blessings. Therefore, we have to be in constant prayer and constantly seeking the wisdom of the Lord in order to overcome and fulfill our purpose.

We need the Lord in our lives in order to continue to learn and grow. Without Him, we are lost. We get lost because we lack wisdom and understanding. The Lord is light, and through Him, we must also shine and share our light with others so they may also follow the Lord.

We must give and share everything we've got: money, time, a smile, or a good word. The light of the Lord's presence makes everything around us real.

Ignorance is darkness, and knowledge and understanding are light. There is only one light in the universe. Jesus said He is the light of the world. Let's keep growing, keep learning, and remain teachable. Let's keep our eyes on the Lord. He is the light of the world.

Remember all the teachable moments in our lives and share them with others. The Lord is the light. Let's spread the light through what we do because the presence of the Lord in our lives is manifested in all the things we say and do.

The sun at dusk and the light over the horizon

For God, who commanded the light to shine out of darkness, hath shined in our hearts, to give the light of the knowledge of the glory of God in the face of Jesus Christ.
—2 Corinthians 4:6

CHAPTER 9

Giving Back

My mother was part of a big family. She had four sisters and seven brothers. My mother was especially close with two of her sisters because they were the oldest of my grandfather and his first wife. My grandmother on my mother's side died when my mother and sisters were young. One of my mother's sisters lived in Puerto Rico, and the other one lived in New York City. I spent summers there and made great memories. The other sister was an evangelical pastor's wife. She was a pastor too, and she was teaching the Bible, preaching, and serving the Lord. Many times, she witnessed God's love by giving everything she had to help others.

She studied the Word of God, read constantly, and participated in the life of her husband's church ministry. Their evangelical congregation was part of the United Church of Christ (UCC) denomination. The UCC operated about fifty-five churches in Puerto Rico at the time. My mother and her sisters had special connection to New York City because some of their brothers and sisters lived there. I have many great memories of all of them and their families.

My aunt Anna had a very strong character and was a great witness of the Lord's power, compassion, and love. She was truly a great example of a faithful Christian who produced much fruit. She and my mother shared many things during their lives. They both shared their desire to serve the Lord by teaching Bible studies and Sunday school classes. Auntie Ana had access to many Christian books and publications, which she happily shared with my mother. Among the many books and publications they shared were writings by Dr. Norman Vincent Peale, a pastor at a great church in New York City.

Dr. Peale has been widely criticized in some Christian circles over the years for his secular teachings. However, since I was a child, I have been exposed to some of his works. I have witnessed the good spiritual medicine that Dr. Peale's Bible-inspired works have been to many. His works on the themes of planting, sowing, giving, saving, sharing, enjoying, and generally having a grateful heart have produced hope among many.

These writings are not the product of Dr. Peale's efforts alone; they are the work of the Holy Spirit working in his life and using the seeds the Lord planted in him to grow, serve, and produce much fruit to help others.

Everything in the universe is the Lord's. We are here in this world for a short period of time, and we are called by the Lord to use the seeds He planted in us since birth. As we grow as individuals, we should produce much fruit to be shared with all in need for His glory.

The gifts, skills, and talents the Lord gives us are to be used, nourished, and shared during our lives. Wherever we find ourselves, we are to share with others because everything we have, including this life we were given, belongs to the Lord.

Some years back, I prepared a presentation for a class in my church about stewardship. During the process of preparation, I received a revelation from the Lord about who we are and the things that God gives us in order for us to fulfill our purpose in life.

This is what I learned at that time: We are all seeds. We come from seeds, physically, from our mothers and fathers, and we have also received emotional and spiritual seeds since our birth.

- Finding My Purpose, Finding My Way in Life -

When my daughters were young, I was a counselor to a youth group at the church I was attending. We went on camping trips and generally sought activities that made us get in touch with nature and in touch with God's creation: lakes, rivers, mountains, and the sea. We observed the birds and other animals in trying to understand and be appreciative of all the beauty and marvelous things the Lord has made. We talked about this subject quite often.

God is all around us and in us. On one occasion, we went on a trip to climb a mountain. Almost at the top on the mountain, we found a landing place with a big old mango tree. The tree, although large, was easy to climb because it had some branches that were close to the ground. It seemed natural that we would all climb the tree. It was something we all did without even thinking.

By the time I realized all the youngsters had climbed the mango tree and had found spots on different branches and were comfortable, I thought, *Let's pray*. We all prayed and gave thanks to the Lord for the opportunity to be there as one with His creation and with Him. Each member of the group had an opportunity to pray. We cried as we prayed because we truly felt the presence of the Holy Spirit in us and among us.

A great vision came upon me that the tree was Jesus Christ, and we were the fruit of the tree. We were seeds that come from the Lord. We come from seeds, and we produce seeds with what we do in life and the way we go about lives giving to others and sharing the goodness of what the Lord gives us.

During that spiritual experience on that beautiful day, I learned that among all the blessings we receive from the Lord, we receive gifts, talents, things we like to do, and things we are good at. These are the seeds the Lord gives us to plant in fertile soil and grow and multiply.

The book of Matthew contains the parable of the talents:

> For the kingdom of heaven is as a man travelling into a far country, who called his own servants, and

> delivered unto them his goods. And unto one he gave five talents, to another two, and to another one; to every man according to his several ability; and straightway took his journey. (Matthew, 25:14–15)

God gives us all according to His will, our capabilities, and the God-given gifts we develop. In the same way, we have the responsibility before the Lord to be good stewards and grow and develop our talents for His glory. We can only accomplish our full potential when we develop an intimate relationship with our Father through prayer, meditation, study of His Word, and living according to His will.

I learned early in my life that scientifically, when we plant a seed in the earth, care for that seed by keeping it free of weeds, provide water, make sure animals do not uncover the seed and eat it, and use fertile soil, the seed will grow to its full potential by producing fruit. Our lives develop in many similar ways.

It all starts in our minds—with our thoughts and ideas. Our minds are fertile ground. We can choose to plant good seeds of possibility, faith, and hope or cultivate fear and despair, which is what the evil one and others in this world want us to do. This is so critical to understand, and it has to be repeated over and over. We must maintain constant awareness of it.

Growth can be defined many ways. Growth is a process, it is an increase, it is expansion, and it is an act or a manner of becoming. It is God's will that we grow as individuals by developing our skills, gifts, and talents so we can honor Him and serve Him by reaching out and touching nature, which is God's work. God wants us to touch nature with love and care. Touching nature all around us means we become aware of our surroundings and help those we find on ours path and require assistance. It means reaching out and touching and helping all of creation.

Among the many gifts we receive from the Lord is the opportunity to find understanding by seeking wisdom from the

Lord. James explains that whenever we face situations that require growing our understanding through wisdom from the Lord, all we have to do is ask—and then we will receive it (James 1:5–6). God is the fountain of all knowledge and wisdom. He wants us to cultivate our faith, which is certainty, and conviction of the things we are waiting for and cannot see but know are there.

> If any of you lack wisdom, let him ask of God, that giveth to all men liberally, and upbraideth not; and it shall be given him. But let him ask in faith, nothing wavering. For he that wavereth is like a wave of the sea driven with the wind and tossed. (James 1:5–6)

Giving back is an exchange with the universe, which is God's creation. There are many examples of this process illustrated in the Bible, and I see this process clearly in the story of the widow of Zarephath:

> For thus saith the Lord God of Israel, The barrel of meal shall not waste, neither shall the cruse of oil fail, until the day that the Lord sendeth rain upon the earth. And she went and did according to the saying of Elijah: and she, and he, and her house, did eat many days. (1 Kings 17:14–15)

This story is about faith, trusting the Lord's promises, and acting firmly in a spirit of obedience. We must submit to the Lord's will, unconditionally, and surrender before the Lord. When we act in this manner, we will certainly experience the awesome power and love of our Father.

The widow gave herself and all she had. She followed the instructions of the prophet. According to this story, we do not know the circumstances of the widow. All we know for sure is that she was a widow and had a son. The scripture says she only had a little flour and some oil. She gave everything she had to care for the prophet Elijah. In giving everything she had, she was trusting the Lord's promises. She did not question the Lord's direction. This is exactly what the Lord asks from us in every situation. When we give everything to serve others, we will receive what the Lord promises, which are blessings from heaven in whichever way the Lord determines, according to His will. We will witness miracles all around us. We will witness amazing and marvelous things all around us as our Lord expresses His infinite love and power. This is exactly what the widow experienced.

This miracle is similar to what Jesus did in the story of the multiplication of the fish and bread. These are clear demonstrations of God manifesting His power in all things. These miracles altered material things as we normally know them. His love and Power provide for our basic necessities in a supernatural way.

God loves us, and He will provide all the resources—whatever we require—for us to grow and help others grow. By growing and giving along the way, we give back to God's creation. We contribute to God's purpose. We do the Lord's work. We become instruments of the Lord's plans and provisions—even when we think what we have is too small to make a difference. The Lord knows all things, and He will guide us to contribute when we surrender. He will use what we have, no matter what it is, to make extraordinary things happen.

It is God's will that we share the fruits of our growth with others in everything we do and help others grow.

We must help the doctor, the nurse, the fire fighter, the teacher, the mother, the father, the plumber, the computer programmer, the manager, the pastor, the pilot, the soldier, the sailor, the marine, the actor, the musician, the dancer, the athlete, the accountant, the lawyer, the logistician, the supply chain manager, the politician, the newsperson, the sons, the daughters, and the bus drivers in whichever role we are called to serve and contribute to the universe.

When we all give back to God's creation, we contribute to God's glory and fulfill His will all around us.

I have had experiences where I have given back and witnessed the awesome power and love of the Lord manifesting in my life. During one period of my life, I had only twenty or thirty dollars in my checking account. During this particular difficult time of my life, I was immersed in prayer and meditation.

As I came closer to the Lord, I felt the presence of the Holy Spirit in my life. I received a calling from the Lord to take most of what I had and write a check to my pastor for twenty dollars. I did not write the check to the church; I wrote it to my pastor. I did as I was called to do.

The next morning, the pastor came by my mother's house—and she gave him the check. The pastor praised the Lord right there because he was on his way to visit a prisoner and to take the prisoner's wife there as an act of kindness in his ministry in our neighborhood. He used the twenty dollars for gasoline to do this act of kindness.

I did not know any of those details, but the Lord knew because He knows all things. The twenty-dollar gift, a small amount, was a blessing to the pastor and to the family of the prisoner. As it turns out, it was a great blessing to me as well. I was generous and felt the joy of giving.

The next day, I received a check for more than a thousand dollars from a totally unrelated matter and source. Some may dismiss this as just a coincidence, but it was the Lord's will at work. It was a supernatural event as a result of the fact that I answered the call and trusted the Lord. It was the Lord's work, and a blessing from Him came.

The miracle of plowing and preparing the land for planting seeds, working the land, and making sure the seeds grow, multiply, and produce fruit can be compared to many things in life. I like to say that it can be easily compared to the process of preparing to learn a trade or a profession to later earn a living and fulfill our purpose in life. It can also be compared to the process of developing ideas and starting a new business to go on and earn a living and make a contribution to society.

The process of going to school, studying, obtaining knowledge, getting a degree or a certificate, preparing to get a job to earn our living, growing, and contributing to society is the same as plowing a field, planting the seeds, and caring for this field until we reap the harvest of what we planted.

All the resources are gifts from God. The land, seeds, water, time, and energy we require to make it happen all are gifts from God. The Lord will always provide us with the resources we require to accomplish His will in our lives:

The Lord is my shepherd; I shall not want. (Psalm 23)

I will always have what I need. Whatever resources I require to go to college, get a degree, start a business, learn a trade, or otherwise do to prepare to serve and do the Lord's will in my life, the Lord will provide. All we have to do is seek the Lord in prayer, meditation, and fasting so the Lord's will may be revealed to me. My responsibility from that moment on are to be obedient, take action, and do what I am called to do. This requires total and absolute commitment. The Lord wants us to be successful and achieve extraordinary things so we can have what we need and share everything we have. We are witnesses of God's love, power, wisdom, and everlasting life.

This is so very important to understand. All the things we receive from the Lord are gifts and demonstrations of the Lord's everlasting love:

- The land is a gift from God.
- The air we breathe is a gift from God.
- The seeds and gifts we receive are gifts from God.
- Time is a gift from God.
- Health is a gift from God.
- Knowledge and wisdom are gifts from God.

- Families and relationships are gifts from God.
- The life we were given at birth is a gift from God.
- Jesus's life, which was given so we could receive forgiveness and eternal life, is a gift from God.

We are stewards of all these great treasures we receive from God. As managers and administrators, we are called upon to make sure we appreciate and care for all the gifts received and use them for the Lord's glory. God's will is that we share everything we receive to help others. We are called to give back everything we receive.

The Lord promises that His resources will never run out

> The Lord God of Israel: The bin of flour shall not be used up, nor shall the jar of oil run dry. (1 Kings 17:14–15)

The process of working the land, planting the seeds, and caring for the plants requires a lot of dedication, hard work, and focus until the land is ready to be harvested. It requires faith, trust in what we are doing, and confidence that what we have done is going to produce good results. This process is part of giving back. When we do all these things, we experience an increase. This increase is to be shared with others in many ways. The increase will accumulate over time, and that is how riches develop. These resources are not meant to be stored someplace; they are meant to be shared all around us. This is God's will.

Everything belongs to the Lord. Our life is His. Therefore, we are entrusted with resources that are too big for us to really comprehend:

> Thine, O Lord is the greatness, and the power, and the glory, and the victory, and the majesty: for all that is in the heaven and in the earth is thine; thine is the kingdom, O Lord, and thou art exalted as

head above all. Both riches and honour come of thee, and thou reignest over all; and in thine hand is power and might; and in thine hand it is to make great, and to give strength unto all. Now therefore, our God, we thank thee, and praise thy glorious name. But who am I, and what is my people, that we should be able to offer so willingly after this sort? for all things come of thee, and of thine own have we given thee. (Chronicles 29:11–14)

Of all that the Lord provides to us, we are called to give to Him and His creation.

Thank You, Lord, for your infinite blessings and all your love for me and the rest of humanity.

Achievement—hand with graduation ring

CHAPTER 10

Living Your Life Full of Joy

I developed a habit of expressing my gratefulness to the Lord immediately after I jump out of bed and start to prepare for my new day. Every new day in our lives is a gift from God. I make an effort every day to enjoy this precious gift in every moment. We should all fill our hearts and minds with thoughts of gratefulness. This brings joy because it reminds us of God's love for us and all His creation. It is essential to start each new day full of joy. Therefore, I am grateful:

- Thanks for a new day.
- Thanks for having a warm bed to rest in.
- Thanks for having a healthy breakfast.
- Thanks for running water.
- Thanks for the good clothing I enjoy to protect me from the cold in the winter and the heat in the summer.
- Thanks for the parents You gave me, Lord.
- Thanks for my beautiful daughters.
- Thanks for my granddaughters and my grandsons.
- Thanks for my sisters, my brothers, and their families.
- Thanks for my cousins in New York City, Florida, California, Ponce, and San Juan.

- Finding My Purpose, Finding My Way in Life -

Thanks, God, for the opportunity to go to elementary school, middle school, high school, college, and postgraduate schools. All this learning expanded my senses and gave me an opportunity to be aware of my surroundings and the meaning of things.

Thanks for all my mother's teachings about the Bible, the Word of God, because it opened up an infinite source of truth, love, and power—and her passion and dedication to teaching.

Thanks, God, for my grandparents. I leaned so many things from them: compassion, dedication, unconditional love, passion and commitment to the Lord, and the gift of teaching.

Thanks, God, for my father's teachings about work ethic, the ability to dream, and working hard to achieve great things in life. He taught me so many things that have brought joy to my life, especially about machines and the automobile, which are tremendous gifts from God.

Thanks, God, for my humble and magnificent automobile, a great tool to go to work every day and to have fun on weekends traveling to beautiful places the Lord created.

Thanks for my job and all the beautiful people the Lord placed in this organization and this great opportunity to serve—even as we face many conflicts because evil is in the hearts of some. Thanks for the opportunity to pray for those for refusing to see and respect other people's point of view. May we pray for God's forgiveness for them and for the ability to share with them that we can do good even as others persecute us because they disagree with our values and ways of life.

Thanks for the opportunity to greet all my coworkers and executives with joy and share my source of joy every morning.

Thanks for the tools we are able to use at work. They might not be the best, but You entrusted us to do the best we can with what we have available to accomplish our mission.

Thanks, God, for opening paths to obtain and develop better computer systems that extend and expand our ability to do great things as we serve others.

Thanks for the opportunity to support a great group of researchers, scientists, and other great individuals as they look for ways to continue to combat illness and improve the health of our nation and the world.

Thanks for our leadership, which continues to provide direction and the resources we require.

Thanks for the great avenues, bridges, trains, and planes that allow us to go to work and return safely every day.

Thanks for the opportunity to exercise in the afternoons and evenings and walk in such beautiful scenery. As I exercise, I can enjoy the beautiful lakes, rivers, birds, trees, deer, squirrels, and neighbors who use the trails and enjoy such great experiences. Thank You, Lord, for being able to walk in the morning and evening in this environment and witness your amazing sunrise and sunset. Thanks for the rain and the snow, which you made beautiful and necessary for life.

Thanks, God, for the opportunity to come to my place and enjoy the company of my wife and her dog, Diego. We share dinner together, pray together, have great conversations, and make plans for the future. Thanks for Diego's life as I remember him with love and remember how throughout his life I experienced of all other dogs and animals you gifted me with. What a joy!

Thank You, Lord, for every moment of my life and the air I breathe. Thank You for all the resources you place in my hands every day. Thank You, Lord, because you grant me the desires of my heart.

Thank You for the influence of other godly men and women from whom I learned to place my life every day in your hands: "I place this day, my life, my loved ones, my work in the Lord's hands. There is no harm in the Lord's hands, only good. Whatever happens, whatever results, if I am in the Lord's hands it is the Lord's will and it is good" (Norman Vincent Peale, *The Power of Positive Thinking*).

Thank You, Lord, because Your Word teaches us about joy, and I have learned to seek Your presence in my life in such a way that I rejoice in your presence:

- Finding My Purpose, Finding My Way in Life -

> This is the day which the Lord has made; we shall rejoice and be glad in it. (Psalm 118:24)

Thank You, Lord, for understanding that the ultimate joy comes from being in Your presence and acknowledge Your supreme power and authority:

> But the fruit of the Spirit is love, joy, peace, long suffering (patience), gentleness, goodness, faith. (Galatians 5:22)

I found many sources of affirmation about the benefits of being joyful, positive, and optimistic. I learned that we can make a sincere effort through developing habits to be positive and happy. Today is the present, and it is a present from the Lord. Once we learn who we are and what we aspire to be, and focus on being positive, grateful, and happy with who we are today, we can work to change our reality and our circumstances. In fact, when we are positive and happy today, we are able to increase our energy levels, increase our intelligence by improving our perception of all our senses, perform significantly better, increase our creativity, and improve our overall effectiveness.

From the studies that led to *The Happiness Advantage*, it is scientifically established that our brains are 31 percent more productive as a result of being positive and happy. UBS and KPMG are two large companies where the ideas of this book were tested.

These principles are part of "Positive Psychology," which is being taught at Harvard University.

We have choices in life. Every waking moment, we are making decisions about what to do and what not to do. We can focus on the positive or focus on the negative. It is a personal choice. We are free to choose. However, what we chose to think and talk about impacts our reality and our circumstances.

Merriam-Webster defines joy in two parts:

- The emotion evoked by well-being, success, or good fortune or by the prospect of possessing what one desires.
- The expression or exhibition of such emotion; state of happiness or felicity; a source or cause of delight.

The things of this world can bring about joy. However, the joys of this world are temporary. There is nothing wrong with success in the world, which may bring about joy: a son or a daughter, a graduation, a new job, a trip or a vacation, a new car, a new house, or giving to someone in need. However, the only lasting, eternal joy comes as the result of the Lord's presence in our lives. He is everything: the source of the truth, the way, and the life, which are the true sources of joy.

Thank You, Lord, for the great opportunity to start working at the First National Bank of Chicago in 1977 as a grade-four bank operations clerk when I was honorably discharged from the US Army. Thank You for being able to finish my bachelor's degree under the GI Bill and then being promoted eleven times over many years until I became an officer of this great institution, First Chicago Corporation.

Thank You, Lord, for the gift of music. Music is a source of joy to our hearts

> Make a joyful noise unto the Lord, all ye lands (all the Earth). Serve the Lord with gladness: come before his presence with singing. Know ye that the Lord he is God: it is he that hath made us, and not we ourselves; we are his people, and the sheep of his pasture. Enter into his gates with thanksgiving, and into his courts with praise: be thankful unto him, and bless his name. For the Lord is good; his mercy is everlasting; and his truth endureth to all generations. (Psalm 100:1–5)

- Finding My Purpose, Finding My Way in Life -

Thank You for the opportunity to enjoy watching so many great musicians and bands live so many times. Thanks for the opportunity to enjoy great live performances, such as the great band leader, composer, and piano player from the great historical city of Ponce and New York City: Mr. Eddie Palmieri, and Mr. Poncho Sanchez and his Latin Jazz band from Los Angeles.

Thank You, Lord, for the joy of learning to play my electric bass and my Latin rhythm instruments. Thank You for enjoying looking at famous musical instruments from famous American musicians, such as the famous bent trumpet of Mr. John Birks, Dizzy Gillespie, the conga drums of Cuban great Ramon "Mongo" Santamaria, and the beautiful guitar of Prince on display at the Smithsonian National Museum of American History.

Music is culture. Music is an expression from our hearts and souls. This is what I know. Music is a method of communication. It is a method of expressing the deep emotions of our hearts and souls. Ethnomusicologists are individuals who study music and how it is expressed by different groups and societies around the world. Some say that we all have the ability to make music in some way. Music is organized sound that makes sense to the individuals or groups in societies. I know the Lord gave me this gift so I can have joy in my soul through music.

Patrick Burke wrote about ethnomusicologists in *Humanities* in January/February 2015:

> Ethnomusicologists often take pride in having opened up academic music programs, long dominated by European "classical" music, to musical traditions from all over the world. Perhaps another important role that ethnomusicology can play is to encourage all of us to be less afraid of our own capacity for music-making and more willing to make sounds for the sheer joy and conviviality of it. There's certainly ample precedent for the idea, from

Psalm 100 ("Make a joyful noise unto the Lord, all ye lands"—King James version—Public domain) to Walt Whitman's "Song of Myself" ("I sound my barbaric yawp over the roofs of the world") to, for those of us raised on Sesame Street, Joe Raposo's classic song "Sing" ("Don't worry that it's not good enough for anyone else to hear—sing, sing a song!")

Whatever your source of inspiration, ethnomusicology demonstrates that making music is a fundamental part of what it means to be human. Ethnomusicologist Bonnie Wade said, "Every known group of people in the world exercises their creative imaginations to organize sound in some way that is different from the way they organize sound for speech." Make an effort to cultivate your musical gift and make a joyful noise to the Lord. Enjoy serving and worshipping the Lord. We will then experience joy from doing joyful noises for the Lord.

I believe we can experience joy by doing the Lord's will in all the things we do in life. President Lincoln's Gettysburg address moves me for the statement he makes about the importance of the brave soldiers who died at the Battle of Gettysburg. They died for a bigger cause. They bravely gave their lives so our nation could move toward the principle that God and our founders desired from the start: the joy of freedom and the government by the people, for the people and by the people:

> But, in a larger sense, we cannot dedicate—we cannot consecrate—we cannot hallow—this ground. The brave men, living and dead, who struggled here, have consecrated it, far above our poor power to add or detract. The world will little note, nor long remember what we say here, but it can never forget what they did here. It is for us the living, rather, to be dedicated here to the unfinished work

Finding My Purpose, Finding My Way in Life

which they who fought here have thus far so nobly advanced. It is rather for us to be here dedicated to the great task remaining before us—that from these honored dead we take increased devotion to that cause for which they gave the last full measure of devotion—that we here highly resolve that these dead shall not have died in vain—that this nation, under God, shall have a new birth of freedom—and that government of the people, by the people, for the people shall not perish from the earth.

There is joy in understanding the commitment that those soldiers were willing to make—to whatever end was required. Even death could not stop such commitment, and through this effort and sacrifice, we who came after them may find joy in our lives, on this land, in this beloved community of ours.

Joy comes from finding what we love and making the decision to follow what is in our hearts. Even more joy come from committing ourselves to do whatever is necessary to make it happen. When we give it all we've got, God's will becomes our will—and we have harmony in our lives.

Love what you Do. This is what Steve Jobs said during his commencement speech in 2005 at Stanford University. He spoke clearly about his experiences and how he followed his heart to discover his purpose in life. I never had an opportunity to meet Steve Jobs personally, but I feel like I known Steve all my life. I own several books and magazines about Steve Jobs and the Apple brand. We are the same age. I followed the trajectory of Steve Jobs all my adult life.

Steve Jobs talked about the subject of finding what we are supposed to do in life and the joy we can find as a result of finding this role in life.

For me, it was a difficult path to find what I was supposed to do in life. I liked doing different things. I experienced tremendous confusion in my life. For a long time, I was not really sure what I could do in life.

I now understand that I had many paths I could have followed. It is important to understand the joy that will come as a result of trusting our hearts and following our hearts to find and develop our purpose in life.

Life is full of moments and events that help shape our path forward. Many times, things happen to us that we do not realize help prepare us for better and bigger things. It is very important to understand that all through life, we are learning and developing for the next steps toward the realization of our dreams and hopes in our hearts. There is tremendous joy in understanding that even things that may seem difficult are really part of our preparation for a better tomorrow. It is critical to be in touch with our inner calling, which will help us formulate our way forward. When we move forward with joy, confident that we love what we are doing, we find inner peace, which will lead to even greater enlightenment and understanding of who we are and how we fit in the universe and our purpose.

Looking at your dreams is similar to looking at another person. A boy is looking at a girl he has never seen before—or perhaps there are new circumstances—and there is something special about her. These are not just chemical experiences—as some people may explain them—a spiritual dimension touches our hearts. We know, in our hearts, that it is important to pursue that person to learn what it would be like to know them better and formulate a significant life experience for both individuals. These experiences should lead to a joyful path. Even if we experience pain, it can be a path to joy.

Following our hearts to find our purpose it is meant to be a joyful process.

We have to keep looking until we discover our purpose and our reason for being on this planet. There is a reason. It is harder for some people than it is for others. However, for each one of us, it is unique, and we have a duty to bring it to reality.

- Finding My Purpose, Finding My Way in Life -

I have learned from my own personal experience and from other sources, that it is up to us to build the path toward the future we want to happen. In *The Psychology of Winning*, Dr Denis Waitley says that some individuals think that people who win in life—by achieving important things in life—do so because they are lucky. However, this is simply not true. Individuals who achieve important things in life—getting a degree, starting a business, buying a house, developing a career, or serving others—do not achieve these great things because they are lucky. Luck or chance has nothing to do with it. Individuals with high achievements do so because they plan and prepare to get what they want. Then they continue to work, plan, and prepare so they are ready to act when opportunities come. You can take that to the bank.

Life is a challenging adventure. It is up to us to think, plan, and act in a constructive way, positively, with optimism, in order to be in harmony with God's will and conquer and attain our purpose. Amen.

The joy of having faith in the Lord brings about a certainty that, no matter what, the Lord will be there with us. Nothing will separate us from the Lord's love and blessings; we are more than conquerors:

> For I am persuaded, that neither death, nor life, nor angels, nor principalities, nor powers, nor things present, nor things to come, Nor height, nor depth, nor any other creature, shall be able to separate us from the love of God, which is in Christ Jesus our Lord. (Romans 8:38–39)

We are blessed to have many extraordinary individuals who made tremendous contributions to society. Many have left behind a legacy and message of service to others, just like Jesus Christ left us His teachings. Of particular interest and importance are Jesus's messages on serving others and finding joy and blessings in doing so.

We are here to serve the Lord. And we serve the Lord by helping

His creation with whatever we decide to do in life. In doing this, we will find the ultimate joy. We are here to serve our brothers and sisters. The ultimate source of joy is serving God by doing His will and becoming all the great things He has in store for us.

Life is difficult. There are plenty of dragons and other monsters along the roads of life. However, the most formidable adversary we will find is us—and the ideas we build in our minds. There is plenty of negativity in the world, and many people want to influence our behaviors in one way or another. Many will try to use fear to intimidate us. The opinions of others do not determine who we are. My relationship with God determines who I am and what and who I become in life. Therefore, we must have a clear picture of the good things we want to accomplish in life and not focus on what we fear.

We become what we think about most. All achievements in life start with a thought or an idea in our minds. We have the capacity and the ability to transform thoughts into real things. This is a God-given gift.

The source of all abundance, all power, and all wisdom is our Lord Jesus Christ. Seek Him, and you will find everlasting love and power to realize your purpose in life. This is the ultimate source of joy and fulfillment.

I have to make every effort to understand and take the necessary steps to find and fulfill my purpose. It is my own individual responsibility to create the circumstances in life that will lead me to realize my purpose, goals, and objectives.

This is accomplished only through my personal and intimate relationship with God. This is my source of life and joy. My duty is to develop a life of service and joy by serving others. As I do, I will receive abundant blessings beyond my expectations. Psalm 23:5c says, "My cup runneth over." That means that my cup is overflowing, and I have what I need and more. This means abundance:

- Finding My Purpose, Finding My Way in Life -

Thou preparest a table before me in the presence of mine enemies: thou anointest my head with oil; my cup runneth over. Surely goodness and mercy shall follow me all the days of my life:, and I will dwell in the house of the Lord for ever. (Psalm 23:5–6)

Believe

Seek the Lord in all we do, and we will have Joy in all things in life. Find Joy in what we do to serve others, as we serve others we will be serving the Lord and be rewarded abundantly.

CHAPTER 11

Believe

These are the foundations of whatever we achieve during our lives. However, it all starts with what we believe.

There are many ways we can develop our own ways to achieve success in life. However, the following ideas are *the three pillars of achievement*.

The first component of these three pillars is mindset. This is defined by *Merriam Webster* as "mental attitude or inclination." According to Dr. Carol Dweck (17), we either have a fixed mindset or a growth mindset.

The fixed mindset is the belief that I am already all I can be or do, right now, and it does not matter what type of effort I make. I cannot improve upon who I am, as dictated by life, society, and my circumstances.

The growth mindset is based on the belief that my basic qualities are things that I can learn to cultivate through my efforts, strategies, and the help of others. Although people are different in many ways, we all have the ability to change, improve, and grow through hard work, dedication, and clearly defined goals and aspirations.

What kind of mindset I decide to cultivate is my choice. It is my personal decision to focus my thoughts, words, and actions to determine what I become. However, the growth mindset will help us expand our consciousness and push toward making all things possible with joy.

I borrowed this concept from one of my mentors, the internationally renowned author and speaker, Mr. Les Brown: Practice OQP (only quality people). This concept is grounded in the fact that the influence of other people has a tremendous impact of who we are and what we accomplish in life. We need to seek to be around quality people who choose to focus on the possibilities of a better outcome in life and work to improve themselves to be able to do better and help others.

The third pillar of success is communication skills. In order to grow and accomplish our goals, it is essential that we identify the habits that we need to change or improve in order to communicate effectively. This means developing the habits and skills necessary to effectively expressing ideas and develop the skills and processes to transmit information to other individuals through common systems, such as written words or spoken words, and though our everyday behaviors.

Our Creator gave us the ability to impact and change our realities. We have the ability to change our circumstances. This is not limited to the wealthy, the famous, or the strong. The Lord, in His infinite wisdom and love for us, made sure that all of us have what is required to change our circumstances. The Lord gave us a formula: believing (50 percent), planning (25 percent) and executing (25 percent). It is a mathematical equation.

This is not my original idea. A lot of people have written about this since long before Jesus came to Earth. In modern society, many important writers have written extensively about this subject. Many of our leaders in politics, business, academia, and sports have used this formula to achieve extraordinary things. I subscribe to this philosophy and have made it my own.

President Theodore Roosevelt said, "Believe, and you will be halfway there."

It all starts with thoughts and ideas. We take these ideas,

- Finding My Purpose, Finding My Way in Life -

verbalize them, and write about them. Once we say what we say, the words tend to become real.

Merriam Webster defines *believe* as something "to consider to be true or honest, to accept the word or evidence of, to accept something as true, genuine, or real; to have a firm conviction as to the goodness, efficacy, or ability of something."

In this definition, we find powerful words that are impactful and define the act of believing. To believe is to have conviction and to accept something as true and real.

The Old Testament is also known as the Jewish Holy Book or Hebrew Bible. Many scholars divide it into the books of God's Law, the prophets, and writings. Psalm 37 was written by King David. An imperfect man of God, David expressed that as we seek a common union with God, we receive knowledge, wisdom, courage, and enlightenment to define our purpose and manifest that purpose in our lives. Therefore, as we do good things in life and become extensions of the Lord's will all around us, we receive blessings beyond what we could ever imagine:

> Trust in the Lord, and do good; so shalt thou dwell in the land, and verily thou shalt be fed. Delight thyself also in the Lord:, and he shall give thee the desires of thine heart. (Psalm 37:3–4)

Earl Nightingale was a published author, radio personality, and publishing executive of Nightingale Conant Corporation. He, among other important things, recorded and published a record entitled *The Strangest Secret*. It was the first spoken word message to selling more than a million copies.

Mr. Nightingale affirms that we become what we think about most. In addition, he establishes that as a result of our focus and concentration of our thoughts on a particular objective, we are able to develop and clearly define goals. Furthermore, people with goals succeed because they know where they're going.

A person's attitude is defined as "a settled way of thinking or feeling about someone or something, typically one that is reflected in a person's behavior" (4). Clear and critical thinking will shape our views of the universe and life in general. Clear and critical thinking will help us confront conflicting situations and develop solutions that bring about growth, understanding, prosperity, and goodness.

Thinking is a gift from our Creator. Creative thinking is imagination. Imagination is being able to think about the future, the things we would like to become real in our lives, and being able to see ourselves actually having and experiencing these ideas, concepts, or dreams. Imagination is a gift that we all have. Some individuals are able to develop the skill of using imagination to help them walk through life and build a better life.

The most important thing for us in our lives is to seek the truth in all we do and all we believe, every day. This is a tremendous challenge, especially as we face tons of information and opinions from so many sources. Now, more than ever, it is critical that we make every effort to understand what is true and real. Old-fashioned values of honesty, goodwill, hope, optimism, love, and compassion for all things created are eternal, and they will act as a guide or path to great accomplishments for serving many and being a good steward of creation. We exist to serve. This is our purpose.

The law of cause and effect is Newton's famous third law of motion: for every action, there is a reaction. This is a law of physics, and it applies to everything in the universe. Our thoughts are things. We are born with the God-given ability to transform our thoughts into real things. This is a very important process to understand to realize how critical it is to focus our thoughts on our goals and objectives. By directing our energy into our thoughts, we are able to create a path toward the realization of our goals, objectives, and purpose.

Financially and otherwise, our contributions to the universe determine what and how we are rewarded. This is also established by the universal law of reciprocity: the golden rule. As we do to others, and we plant seeds in life, so we sow. In the same manner as we plant seeds in the ground, and in due time, a plant will grow. We will sow in a multiplied way. This is the same when we give a smile, a helping hand, or a dollar to feed the hungry. This is planting good deeds and goodwill. This is part of our purpose in life; by doing this, we share the blessings received with the universe all around us.

When we set aside money for any particular purpose, we call it savings. This is one of many ways to manage the available resources of the universe, our resources, by investing for the future: a car, a house, or college. If we save $100 a week, for a year, at the end of the first year, we will have $5,200. If we invest this $5,200 at 5 percent annual interest, at the end of the first year, we will have $5,466.04. In other words, our money would have earned $266.04. If we continue our program of putting in $100 every week and do not use that money, we will have $11,211.69 at the end of the second period. In other words, our money would have earned $811.69 in interest. This is an example of why savings is so critical for building financial freedom. This is an example of manifesting an idea through a specific plan and purpose and how our resources can be cultivated to manifest those things in our hearts and minds—into the world of the possible. If we continue this program for ten years, we will have way more than sixty thousand dollars, which we can invest to continue to grow our resources and expand and manifest our dreams.

What we do at work has the effect as in the example of planting seeds and savings. As we do to serve others well, we will receive rewards we can imagine and beyond. We must make every effort to be amazing to the people we serve. This is the key to success in whatever we choose to do in life.

God's will is that we commit to serve Him by learning His purpose for us in life. This requires, among many things, investing time and effort and other resources on improving ourselves and building a future serving the Lord by serving others. Amen.

Be yourself. Be the unique individual God created you to be. Go out into the world, achieve, and do great things to help others—and you will be blessed abundantly,

> For as he thinks in his heart, so is he.
> —Proverbs 23:7a

REFERENCES

1. The Bible (King James Version). (1960). United Bible Societies, www.biblegateway.com, retrieved July 28, 2013.
2. Apter, T. (1997). *The Confident Child.* New York, NY: W.W. Norton and Company, Inc.
3. Covey, S. (1998). *The 7 Habits of Highly Effective Teens.* New York: Simon and Schuster, Fireside.
4. Rodgers, B. and. (1987). *Getting the Best Out of Yourself and Others.* New York: Harper and Row Publishers.
5. http://www.bls.gov/ooh/business-and-financial/logisticians.htm, retrieved August 9, 2014.
6. Kouzes, J. M and Posner, B. Z. (2007). *The Leadership Challenge* (4th ed.). San Francisco: Jossey-Bass Publishers.
7. http://umaine.edu/publications/4356e/, retrieved August 31, 2014.
8. http://www.ted.com/talks/annie_murphy_paul_what_we_learn_before_we_re_born/transcript?language=en, retrieved August 31, 2014.
9. http://www.nytimes.com/2009/07/12/business/12corner.html?pagewanted=all, retrieved February 17, 2015, "At Yum Brands, Rewards for Good Work," David C. Novak (2009).
10. http://www.yum.com/company/srofficers.asp, retrieved February 17, 2015.
11. http://news.stanford.edu/news/2005/june15/jobs-061505.html, retrieved February 17, 2015—Steve Jobs Commencement Speech (2005).
12. http://www.merriam-webster.com/dictionary/believe, retrieved February 20, 2015.
13. Peale, Norman Vincent (1985); *Enthusiasm Makes the Difference,* Simon and Schuster.
14. http://www.americanrhetoric.com/speeches/mlkihaveadream.htm, retrieved February 17, 2015.

15 Dweck, Carol S., (2006), *Mindset: The New Psychology of Success*, Random House, New York, NY.
16 Hill, Napoleon, (1960), *Think and Grow Rich*, Random House, New York, NY.
17 Ziglar, Zig, (1995), *Goals*, Nightingale-Conant Corporation, Simon and Schuster, Inc., New York, NY.
18 Maxwell, John C. (2006), *The Difference Maker*, Thomas Nelson, Inc., Nashville, Tennessee.
19 http://www.drchristinahibbert.com/personal-growth-and-self-actualization/, retrieved October 25, 2015.
20 http://www.merriam-webster.com/dictionary/self-actualize, retrieved October 25, 2015.
21 Ward, Charles (1990–2015), *Customer Services Excellence*, Chuck Ward and Associates, Inc., Dallas, Texas.
22 https://www.linkedin.com/pulse/why-consciousness-biggest-secret-success-deepak-chopra-md-official, retrieved August 2, 2015.
23 Joy; https://www.merriam-webster.com/dictionary/joy, retrieved January 17, 2017.
24 Abraham Lincoln, "Gettysburg Address" (November 19, 1863), http://www.americaslibrary.gov/jb/civil/jb_civil_gettysbg_3_e.html, retrieved February 19, 2017.
25 http://kingencyclopedia.stanford.edu/encyclopedia/documentsentry/doc_unfulfilled_dreams.1.html, retrieved February 19, 2017.
26 http://news.stanford.edu/2005/06/14/jobs-061505/, retrieved February 19, 2017.
27 https://www.neh.gov/humanities/2015/januaryfebruary/feature/what-music-is—retrieved February 19, 2017, Patrick Burke | HUMANITIES, January/February 2015 | volume 36, number 1.
   (1) https://www.merriam-webster.com/dictionary/believe, retrieved November 29, 2019.
   (3) https://www.nightingale.com/articles/the-strangest-secret/, retrieved November 29, 2019.
   (4) https://www.lexico.com/en, retrieved January 20, 2020.